OSHA 10-Hour
Construction

Student Workbook

Raúl Ross Pineda
compiler

OSHA Outreach Training Program Series

OSHA 10-Hour Construction; Student Workbook
© Raúl Ross Pineda
Chicago, Illinois, USA
V.1 May 2017
V.2 September 2017
V.3 April 2018
ISBN-13: 978-1546484363
ISBN-10: 1546484361

OSHA 10-Hour Construction
Student Workbook

This book contains the handouts for the OSHA Outreach Training Program's 10-Hour Construction course. It includes the pamphlets that highlight the key points to be presented by the instructor, as well as the group activities to be performed and the questionnaires to be answered by the students in class.

This book is a compilation of every pamphlet provided on the OSHA web page dedicated to this course, as reviewed on April 2, 2018.

 Raúl Ross Pineda (mxsinfronteras@gmail.com) has worked for over 30 years in construction and general industry. He is an OSHA Authorized Trainer at the Latino Worker Safety Center (obrerolatino.org).

Content

Introduction to OSHA

Job Safety and Health
IT'S THE LAW!

All workers have the right to:

- A safe workplace.

- Raise a safety or health concern with your employer or OSHA, or report a work-related injury or illness, without being retaliated against.

- Receive information and training on job hazards, including all hazardous substances in your workplace.

- Request an OSHA inspection of your workplace if you believe there are unsafe or unhealthy conditions. OSHA will keep your name confidential. You have the right to have a representative contact OSHA on your behalf.

- Participate (or have your representative participate) in an OSHA inspection and speak in private to the inspector.

- File a complaint with OSHA within 30 days (by phone, online or by mail) if you have been retaliated against for using your rights.

- See any OSHA citations issued to your employer.

- Request copies of your medical records, tests that measure hazards in the workplace, and the workplace injury and illness log.

This poster is available free from OSHA.

Contact OSHA. We can help.

Employers must:

- Provide employees a workplace free from recognized hazards. It is illegal to retaliate against an employee for using any of their rights under the law, including raising a health and safety concern with you or with OSHA, or reporting a work-related injury or illness.

- Comply with all applicable OSHA standards.

- Report to OSHA all work-related fatalities within 8 hours, and all inpatient hospitalizations, amputations and losses of an eye within 24 hours.

- Provide required training to all workers in a language and vocabulary they can understand.

- Prominently display this poster in the workplace.

- Post OSHA citations at or near the place of the alleged violations.

FREE ASSISTANCE to identify and correct hazards is available to small and medium-sized employers, without citation or penalty, through OSHA-supported consultation programs in every state.

Employers Must Provide and Pay for Most PPE

Personal Protective Equipment (PPE)

The Occupational Safety and Health Administration (OSHA) requires that employers protect you from workplace hazards that can cause injury or illness. Controlling a hazard at its source is the best way to protect workers. However, when engineering, work practice and administrative controls are not feasible or do not provide sufficient protection, employers must provide personal protective equipment (PPE) to you and ensure its use.

PPE is equipment worn to minimize exposure to a variety of hazards. Examples include items such as gloves, foot and eye protection, protective hearing protection (earplugs, muffs), hard hats and respirators.

Employer Obligations	Workers should:
✓ Performing a "hazard assessment" of the workplace to identify and control physical and health hazards. ✓ Identifying and providing appropriate PPE for employees. ✓ Training employees in the use and care of the PPE. ✓ Maintaining PPE, including replacing worn or damaged PPE. ✓ Periodically reviewing, updating and evaluating the effectiveness of the PPE program.	✓ Properly wear PPE ✓ Attend training sessions on PPE ✓ Care for, clean and maintain PPE, an ✓ Inform a supervisor of the need to repair or replace PPE.

Employers Must Pay for Personal Protective Equipment (PPE)

On May 15, 2008, a new OSHA rule about employer payment for PPE went into effect. With few exceptions, OSHA now requires employers to pay for personal protective equipment used to comply with OSHA standards. The final rule does not create new requirements regarding what PPE employers must provide.

The standard makes clear that employers cannot require workers to provide their own PPE and the worker's use of PPE they already own must be completely voluntary. Even when a worker provides his or her own PPE, the employer must ensure that the equipment is adequate to protect the worker from hazards at the workplace.

Examples of PPE that Employers Must Pay for Include:

- Metatarsal foot protection
- Rubber boots with steel toes
- Non-prescription eye protection
- Prescription eyewear inserts/lenses for full face respirators
- Goggles and face shields

- Fire fighting PPE (helmet, gloves, boots, proximity suits, full gear)
- Hard hats
- Hearing protection
- Welding PPE

3

HANDOUT #4
Employers Must Provide and Pay for Most PPE

Payment Exceptions under the OSHA Rule

Employers are not required to pay for some PPE in certain circumstances:
- Non-specialty safety-toe protective footwear (including steel-toe shoes or boots) and non-specialty prescription safety eyewear provided that the employer permits such items to be worn off the job site. (OSHA based this decision on the fact that this type of equipment is very personal, is often used outside the workplace, and that it is taken by workers from jobsite to jobsite and employer to employer.)
- Everyday clothing, such as long-sleeve shirts, long pants, street shoes, and normal work boots.
- Ordinary clothing, skin creams, or other items, used solely for protection from weather, such as winter coats, jackets, gloves, parkas, rubber boots, hats, raincoats, ordinary sunglasses, and sunscreen
- Items such as hair nets and gloves worn by food workers for consumer safety.
- Lifting belts because their value in protecting the back is questionable.
- When the employee has lost or intentionally damaged the PPE and it must be replaced.

OSHA Standards that Apply

OSHA General Industry PPE Standards
- 1910.132: General requirements and payment
- 1910.133: Eye and face protection
- 1910.134: Respiratory protection
- 1910.135: Head protection
- 1910.136: Foot protection
- 1910.137: Electrical protective devices
- 1910.138: Hand protection

OSHA Construction PPE Standards
- 1926.28: Personal protective equipment
- 1926.95: Criteria for personal protective equipment
- 1926.96: Occupational foot protection
- 1926.100: Head protection
- 1926.101: Hearing protection
- 1926.102: Eye and face protection
- 1926.103: Respiratory protection

There are also PPE requirements in shipyards and marine terminals and many standards on specific hazards, such as 1910.1030: Bloodborne pathogens and 1910.146: Permit-required confined spaces.

OSHA standards are online at www.osha.gov.

Sources:
- *Employers Must Provide and Pay for PPE, New Jersey Work Environment Council (WEC) Fact Sheet*
- *OSHA Standards, 1910.132(h) and 1926.95(d)*
- *Employer Payment for Personal Protective Equipment Final Rule, Federal Register: November 15, 2007 (Volume 72, Number 220)*

OSHA FactSheet

Your Rights as a Whistleblower

You may file a complaint with OSHA if your employer retaliates against you by taking unfavorable personnel action because you engaged in protected activity relating to workplace safety or health, asbestos in schools, cargo containers, airline, commercial motor carrier, consumer product, environmental, financial reform, food safety, health insurance reform, motor vehicle safety, nuclear, pipeline, public transportation agency, railroad, maritime, and securities laws.

Whistleblower Laws Enforced by OSHA

Each law requires that complaints be filed within a certain number of days after the alleged retaliation.

- *Asbestos Hazard Emergency Response Act* (90 days)
- *Clean Air Act* (30 days)
- *Comprehensive Environmental Response, Compensation and Liability Act* (30 days)
- *Consumer Financial Protection Act of 2010* (180 days)
- *Consumer Product Safety Improvement Act* (180 days)
- *Energy Reorganization Act* (180 days)
- *Federal Railroad Safety Act* (180 days)
- *Federal Water Pollution Control Act* (30 days)
- *International Safe Container Act* (60 days)
- *Moving Ahead for Progress in the 21st Century Act* (motor vehicle safety) (180 days)
- *National Transit Systems Security Act* (180 days)
- *Occupational Safety and Health Act* (30 days)
- *Pipeline Safety Improvement Act* (180 days)
- *Safe Drinking Water Act* (30 days)
- *Sarbanes-Oxley Act* (180 days)
- *Seaman's Protection Act* (180 days)
- *Section 402 of the FDA Food Safety Modernization Act* (180 days)
- *Section 1558 of the Affordable Care Act* (180 days)
- *Solid Waste Disposal Act* (30 days)
- *Surface Transportation Assistance Act* (180 days)
- *Toxic Substances Control Act* (30 days)
- *Wendell H. Ford Aviation Investment and Reform Act for the 21st Century* (90 days)

Unfavorable Personnel Actions

Your employer may be found to have retaliated against you if your protected activity was a contributing or motivating factor in its decision to take unfavorable personnel action against you. Such actions may include:

- Applying or issuing a policy which provides for an unfavorable personnel action due to activity protected by a whistleblower law enforced by OSHA
- Blacklisting
- Demoting
- Denying overtime or promotion
- Disciplining
- Denying benefits
- Failing to hire or rehire
- Firing or laying off
- Intimidation
- Making threats
- Reassignment to a less desirable position, including one adversely affecting prospects for promotion
- Reducing pay or hours
- Suspension

Filing a Complaint

If you believe that your employer retaliated against you because you exercised your legal rights as an employee, contact OSHA as soon as possible because you must file your complaint within the legal time limits.

An employee can file a complaint with OSHA by visiting or calling the local OSHA office or sending a written complaint to the closest OSHA regional or area office. Written complaints may be filed by facsimile, electronic communication, hand delivery during business hours, U.S. mail (confirmation services recommended), or other third-party commercial carrier. The date of the postmark, facsimile, electronic communication, telephone call, hand delivery, delivery to a third-party commercial carrier, or in-person filing at an OSHA office is considered the date filed. No particular form is required and complaints may be submitted in any language.

For OSHA area office contact information, please call 1-800-321-OSHA (6742) or visit www.osha.gov/html/RAmap.html.

Upon receipt of a complaint, OSHA will first review it to determine whether it is valid on its face. All complaints are investigated in accord with the statutory requirements.

With the exception of employees of the U.S. Postal Service, public sector employees (those employed as municipal, county, state, territorial or federal workers) are not covered by the *Occupational Safety and Health Act* (OSH Act). Non-federal public sector employees and, except in Connecticut, New York, New Jersey, the Virgin Islands, and Illinois, private sector employees are covered in states which operate their own occupational safety and health programs approved by Federal OSHA. For information on the 27 State Plan states, call 1-800-321-OSHA (6742), or visit www.osha.gov/dcsp/osp/index.html.

A federal employee who wishes to file a complaint alleging retaliation due to disclosure of a substantial and specific danger to public health or safety or involving occupational safety or health should contact the Office of Special Counsel (www.osc.gov) and OSHA's Office of Federal Agency Programs (www.osha.gov/dep/enforcement/dep_offices.html).

Coverage of public sector employees under the other statutes administered by OSHA varies by statute. If you are a public sector employee and you are unsure whether you are covered under a whistleblower protection statute, call 1-800-321-OSHA (6742) for assistance, or visit www.whistleblowers.gov.

How OSHA Determines Whether Retaliation Took Place

The investigation must reveal that:

- The employee engaged in protected activity;
- The employer knew about or suspected the protected activity;
- The employer took an adverse action; and
- The protected activity motivated or contributed to the adverse action.

If the evidence supports the employee's allegation and a settlement cannot be reached, OSHA will generally issue an order, which the employer may contest, requiring the employer to reinstate the employee, pay back wages, restore benefits, and other possible remedies to make the employee whole. Under some of the statutes the employer must comply with the reinstatement order immediately. In cases under the *Occupational Safety and Health Act, Asbestos Hazard Emergency Response Act,* and the *International Safe Container Act,* the Secretary of Labor will file suit in federal district court to obtain relief.

Partial List of Whistleblower Protections

Whistleblower Protections under the OSH Act

The OSH Act protects workers who complain to their employer, OSHA or other government agencies about unsafe or unhealthful working conditions in the workplace or environmental problems. You cannot be transferred, denied a raise, have your hours reduced, be fired, or punished in any other way because you used any right given to you under the OSH Act. Help is available from OSHA for whistleblowers.

If you have been punished or discriminated against for using your rights, you must file a complaint with OSHA within 30 days of the alleged reprisal for most complaints. No form is required, but you must send a letter or call the OSHA Area Office nearest you to report the discrimination (within 30 days of the alleged discrimination).

You have a limited right under the OSH Act to refuse to do a job because conditions are hazardous. You may do so under the OSH Act only when (1) you believe that you face death or serious injury (and the situation is so clearly hazardous that any reasonable person would believe the same thing); (2) you have tried, where possible, to get your employer to correct the condition, and been unable to obtain a correction and there is no other way to do the job safely; and (3) the situation is so urgent that you do not have time to eliminate the hazard through regulatory channels such as calling OSHA. For details, see www.osha.gov/as/opa/worker/refuse.html. OSHA cannot enforce union contracts or state laws that give employees the right to refuse to work.

Whistleblower Protections in the Transportation Industry

Employees whose jobs directly affect commercial motor vehicle safety or security are protected from retaliation by their employers for, among other things, reporting violations of federal or state commercial motor carrier safety or security regulations, or refusing to operate a vehicle because of violations of federal commercial motor vehicle safety or security regulations or because they have a reasonable apprehension of death or serious injury to themselves or the public and they have sought from the employer and been unable to obtain correction of the hazardous condition.

Similarly, employees of air carriers, their contractors or subcontractors who raise safety concerns or report violations of FAA rules and regulations are protected from retaliation, as are employees of owners and operators of pipelines, their contractors and subcontractors who report violations of pipeline safety rules and regulations. Employees involved in international shipping who report unsafe shipping containers are also protected. In addition, employees of railroad carriers or public transportation agencies, their contractors or subcontractors who report safety or security conditions or violations of federal rules and regulations relating to railroad or public transportation safety or security are protected from retaliation.

Whistleblower Protections for Voicing Environmental Concerns

A number of laws protect employees from retaliation because they report violations of environmental laws related to drinking water and water pollution, toxic substances, solid waste disposal, air quality and air pollution, asbestos in schools, and hazardous waste disposal sites. The *Energy Reorganization Act* protects employees

from retaliation for raising safety concerns in the nuclear power industry and in nuclear medicine.

Whistleblower Protections When Reporting Corporate Fraud

Employees who work for publicly traded companies or companies required to file certain reports with the Securities and Exchange Commission are protected from retaliation for reporting alleged mail, wire, bank or securities fraud; violations of SEC rules or regulations of the SEC; or violations of federal laws relating to fraud against shareholders.

Whistleblower Protections for Voicing Consumer Product Concerns

Employees of consumer product manufacturers, importers, distributors, retailers, and private labelers are protected from retaliation for reporting reasonably perceived violations of any statute or regulation within the jurisdiction of the Consumer Product Safety Commission.

More Information

To obtain more information on whistleblower laws, go to www.whistleblowers.gov.

This is one of a series of informational fact sheets highlighting OSHA programs, policies, or standards. It does not impose any new compliance requirements. For a comprehensive list of compliance requirements of OSHA standards and regulations, refer to Title 29 of the Code of Federal Regulations. Because some of these whistleblower laws have only recently been enacted, the final regulations implementing them may not yet be available in the Code of Federal Regulations but the laws are still being enforced by OSHA. This information will be made available to sensory-impaired individuals upon request. Voice phone number: (202) 693-1999; teletypewriter (TTY) number: (877) 889-5627.

For assistance, contact us. We can help. It's confidential.

U.S. Department of Labor
www.osha.gov (800) 321-OSHA (6742)

DWP FS-3638 04/2013

We Are OSHA

We Can Help

Workers' rights under the OSH Act

Workers are entitled to working conditions that do not pose a risk of serious harm. To help assure a safe and healthful workplace, OSHA also provides workers with the right to:

- Ask OSHA to inspect their workplace;

- Use their rights under the law without retaliation;

- Receive information and training about hazards, methods to prevent harm, and the OSHA standards that apply to their workplace. The training must be in a language you can understand;

- Get copies of test results done to find hazards in the workplace;

- Review records of work-related injuries and illnesses; and

- Get copies of their medical records.

Occupational Safety and Health Administration
U.S. Department of Labor

Who OSHA covers

Private sector workers

Most employees in the nation come under OSHA's jurisdiction. OSHA covers private sector employers and employees in all 50 states, the District of Columbia, and other U.S. jurisdictions either directly through Federal OSHA or through an OSHA-approved state program. State-run health and safety programs must be at least as effective as the Federal OSHA program. To find the contact information for the OSHA Federal or State Program office nearest you, call 1-800-321-OSHA (6742) or go to www.osha.gov.

State and local government workers

Employees who work for state and local governments are not covered by Federal OSHA, but have OSH Act protections if they work in those states that have an OSHA-approved state program. The following 22 states or territories have OSHA-approved programs:

Alaska	Arizona	California
Hawaii	Indiana	Iowa
Kentucky	Maryland	Michigan
Minnesota	Nevada	New Mexico
North Carolina	Oregon	South Carolina
Tennessee	Utah	Vermont
Virginia	Washington	Wyoming
Puerto Rico		

Five additional states and one U.S. territory have OSHA-approved plans that cover public sector workers only:

Connecticut	Illinois	Maine
New Jersey	New York	Virgin Islands

Private sector workers in these five states and the Virgin Islands are covered by Federal OSHA.

Federal government workers

Federal agencies must have a safety and health program that meets the same standards as private employers. Although OSHA does not fine federal agencies, it does monitor federal agencies and responds to workers' complaints. The United States Postal Service (USPS) is covered by OSHA.

Not covered under the OSH Act:
- Self-employed;
- Immediate family members of farm employers who do not employ outside employees;
- Workplace hazards regulated by another federal agency (for example, the Mine Safety and Health Administration, the Department of Energy, or Coast Guard).

OSHA standards: Protection on the job

OSHA standards are rules that describe the methods that employers must use to protect their employees from hazards. There are OSHA standards for Construction work, Agriculture, Maritime operations, and General Industry, which are the standards that apply to most worksites. These standards limit the amount of hazardous chemicals workers can be exposed to, require the use of certain safe practices and equipment, and require employers to monitor hazards and keep records of workplace injuries and illnesses.

Examples of OSHA standards include requirements to provide fall protection, prevent trenching cave-ins, prevent some infectious diseases, assure that workers

safely enter confined spaces, prevent exposure to harmful substances like asbestos, put guards on machines, provide respirators or other safety equipment, and provide training for certain dangerous jobs.

Employers must also comply with the General Duty Clause of the OSH Act, which *requires employers to keep their workplace free of serious recognized hazards*. This clause is generally cited when no OSHA standard applies to the hazard.

Workers can ask OSHA to inspect their workplace

Workers, or their representatives, may file a complaint and ask OSHA to inspect their workplace if they believe there is a serious hazard or that their employer is not following OSHA standards. A worker can tell OSHA not to let their employer know who filed the complaint. **It is a violation of the OSH Act for an employer to fire, demote, transfer or retaliate in any way against a worker for filing a complaint or using other OSHA rights.**

Written complaints that are signed by a worker or their representative and submitted to the closest OSHA office are more likely to result in an on-site OSHA inspection. You can call 1-800-321-OSHA (6742) to request a complaint form from your local OSHA office or visit www.osha.gov/pls/osha7/eComplaintForm.html to submit the form online. Completed forms can also be faxed or mailed to the local OSHA office. Most complaints sent in online may be resolved informally over the phone with your employer.

When the OSHA inspector arrives, workers and their representatives have the right to:

• Go along on the inspection;
• Talk privately with the OSHA inspector; and
• Take part in meetings with the inspector and the employer before and after the inspection is conducted.

Where there is no union or employee representative, the OSHA inspector must talk confidentially with a reasonable number of workers during the course of the investigation.

When an inspector finds violations of OSHA standards or serious hazards, OSHA may issue citations and fines. A citation includes the methods an employer may use to fix a problem and the date by when the corrective actions must be completed. Workers only have the right to challenge the deadline for when a problem must be resolved. Employers, on the other hand, have the right to contest whether there is a violation or any other part of the citation. Workers or their representatives must notify OSHA that they want to be involved in the appeals process if the employer challenges a citation.

If you send in a complaint requesting an OSHA inspection, you have the right to find out the results of the OSHA inspection and request a review if OSHA does not issue citations.

Employer responsibilities

Employers have the responsibility to provide a safe workplace. **Employers MUST provide their employees with a workplace that does not have serious hazards and must follow all OSHA safety and health standards.** Employers must find and correct safety and health problems. OSHA further requires employers to try to eliminate or reduce hazards first by making changes in working conditions rather than just relying on masks, gloves, earplugs or other types of personal protective equipment. Switching to safer chemicals, implementing processes to trap harmful fumes, or using ventilation systems to clean the air are examples of effective ways to get rid of or minimize risks.

Employers **MUST** also:

• Prominently display the official OSHA *Job Safety and Health – It's the Law* poster that describes rights and responsibilities under the OSH Act. **This poster is free and can be downloaded from www.osha.gov.**

• Inform workers about chemical hazards through training, labels, alarms, color-coded systems, chemical information sheets and other methods.

• Provide safety training to workers in a language and vocabulary they can understand.

• Keep accurate records of work-related injuries and illnesses.

• Perform tests in the workplace, such as air sampling, required by some OSHA standards.

• Provide required personal protective equipment at no cost to workers.*

• Provide hearing exams or other medical tests required by OSHA standards.

- Post OSHA citations and injury and illness data where workers can see them.

- Notify OSHA within 8 hours of a workplace fatality or within 24 hours of any work-related inpatient hospitalization, amputation or loss of an eye (1-800-321-OSHA [6742]).

- Not retaliate against workers for using their rights under the law, including their right to report a work-related injury or illness.

* Employers must pay for most types of required personal protective equipment.

The law protects workers from retaliation when using their OSHA rights

The OSH Act protects workers who complain to their employer, OSHA or other government agencies about unsafe or unhealthful working conditions in the workplace or environmental problems. You cannot be transferred, denied a raise, have your hours reduced, be fired, or punished in any other way because you used any right given to you under the OSH Act. Help is available from OSHA for whistleblowers.

If you have been punished or retaliated against for using your rights, you must file a complaint with OSHA **within 30 days** from the date the retaliatory decision was both made and communicated to you. No form is needed, but you must call OSHA within 30 days of the alleged retaliation at 1-800-321-OSHA (6742) and ask to speak to the OSHA area office nearest you to report the retaliation.

You have the right to a safe workplace

The *Occupational Safety and Health Act of 1970* (OSH Act) was passed to prevent workers from being killed or seriously harmed at work. The law requires that employers provide their employees with working conditions that are free of known dangers. The Act created the Occupational Safety and Health Administration (OSHA), which sets and enforces protective workplace safety and health standards. OSHA also provides information, training and assistance to workers and employers. Workers may file a complaint to have OSHA inspect their workplace if they believe that their employer is not following OSHA standards or there are serious hazards.

Contact us if you have questions or want to file a complaint. We will keep your information confidential. We are here to help you. Call our toll-free number at 1-800-321-OSHA (6742) or go to www.osha.gov.

Occupational Safety and Health Administration

U.S. Department of Labor

1-800-321-OSHA (6742)   TTY 1-877-889-5627
www.osha.gov

OSHA 3334-09R 2015

Activity: Ways to Report Workplace Hazards

Instructions

Based on the following scenario, discuss how you would follow the *Ways to Report Workplace Hazards* to determine what reporting approach would be best. Read the questions listed below that when answered, provide the information important to reporting workplace hazards. Is any additional information needed?

Scenario

You are a construction worker for ABC, Inc., 1000 Sweet Road, Anytown, USA, 40001. ABC does non-residential plumbing, heating and air conditioning work. You have worked for ABC for 3 years. You, along with 7 co-workers, have been installing sheet metal ductwork in the lower level of the Anytown Shopping Mall, which is undergoing renovation, for the past few weeks. The site is located in the Northwest quadrant, in the basement of the anchor store, located at 555 Times Drive, in Anytown. One of your coworkers has been operating a 65-horsepower concrete cutting saw in the same area. The saw is being run in the propane mode. You and several coworkers get headaches from the fumes whenever the saw is used and have told your supervisor about the problem. The supervisor said that nothing could be done, because the General Contractor, CAB Management, has control over the site and this job will be complete in another month. You did some research and found out that exposure to propane in a confined, unventilated area can cause headaches, dizziness, difficulty breathing and unconsciousness. There is no ventilation or monitoring of the air in the area. After talking with coworkers, you decide to report the hazards.

Questions

- Has anyone been injured or made ill as a result of this problem?

- How many employees work at the site and how many are exposed to the hazard?

- How and when are workers exposed? On what shifts does the hazard exist?

- What work is performed in the unsafe or unhealthful area?

- What type of equipment is used? Is it in good condition?

- What materials and/or chemicals are used?

- Have employees been informed or trained regarding hazardous conditions?

- What process and/or operation is involved? What kinds of work are done nearby?

- How often and for how long do employees work at the task that leads to their exposure?

- How long (to your knowledge) has the condition existed?

- Have any attempts been made to correct the problem? Have there been any "near-miss" incidents?

Topic 4: Workers Rights Practice Worksheet
Crossword Puzzle

OSHA Provides Workers the Right to:

Across

4. Hazard _____ and medical records

6. Information about _____ and illnesses in your workplace

7. A safe and _____ workplace

8. Complain or request hazard _____ from employer

9. Participate in an OSHA _____

Down

1. Know about _____ conditions

2. Be free from _____ for exercising safety and health rights

3. _____ as provided in the OSHA standards

5. File a complaint with _____

Personal protective
and lifesaving equipment

Personal Protective Equipment

Personal protective equipment, or PPE, is designed to protect workers from serious workplace injuries or illnesses resulting from contact with chemical, radiological, physical, electrical, mechanical, or other workplace hazards. Besides face shields, safety glasses, hard hats, and safety shoes, protective equipment includes a variety of devices and garments such as goggles, coveralls, gloves, vests, earplugs, and respirators.

Employer Responsibilities

OSHA's primary personal protective equipment standards are in Title 29 of the Code of Federal Regulations (CFR), Part 1910 Subpart I, and equivalent regulations in states with OSHA-approved state plans, but you can find protective equipment requirements elsewhere in the General Industry Standards. For example, 29 CFR 1910.156, OSHA's Fire Brigades Standard, has requirements for firefighting gear. In addition, 29 CFR 1926.95-106 covers the construction industry. OSHA's general personal protective equipment requirements mandate that employers conduct a hazard assessment of their workplaces to determine what hazards are present that require the use of protective equipment, provide workers with appropriate protective equipment, and require them to use and maintain it in sanitary and reliable condition.

Using personal protective equipment is often essential, but it is generally the last line of defense after engineering controls, work practices, and administrative controls. Engineering controls involve physically changing a machine or work environment. Administrative controls involve changing how or when workers do their jobs, such as scheduling work and rotating workers to reduce exposures. Work practices involve training workers how to perform tasks in ways that reduce their exposure to workplace hazards.

As an employer, you must assess your workplace to determine if hazards are present that require the use of personal protective equipment. If such hazards are present, you must select protective equipment and require workers to use it, communicate your protective equipment selection decisions to your workers, and select personal protective equipment that properly fits your workers.

You must also train workers who are required to wear personal protective equipment on how to do the following:
- Use protective equipment properly,
- Be aware of when personal protective equipment is necessary,
- Know what kind of protective equipment is necessary,
- Understand the limitations of personal protective equipment in protecting workers from injury,
- Put on, adjust, wear, and take off personal protective equipment, and
- Maintain protective equipment properly.

Protection from Head Injuries

Hard hats can protect your workers from head impact, penetration injuries, and electrical injuries such as those caused by falling or flying objects, fixed objects, or contact with electrical conductors. Also, OSHA regulations require employers to ensure that workers cover and protect long hair to prevent it from getting caught in machine parts such as belts and chains.

Protection from Foot and Leg Injuries

In addition to foot guards and safety shoes, leggings (e.g., leather, aluminized rayon, or other appropriate material) can help prevent injuries by protecting workers from hazards such as falling or rolling objects, sharp objects, wet and slippery surfaces, molten metals, hot surfaces, and electrical hazards.

Protection from Eye and Face Injuries

Besides spectacles and goggles, personal protective equipment such as special helmets or shields, spectacles with side shields, and faceshields can protect workers from the hazards of flying fragments, large chips, hot sparks, optical radiation, splashes from molten metals, as well as objects, particles, sand, dirt, mists, dusts, and glare.

Protection from Hearing Loss
Wearing earplugs or earmuffs can help prevent damage to hearing. Exposure to high noise levels can cause irreversible hearing loss or impairment as well as physical and psychological stress. Earplugs made from foam, waxed cotton, or fiberglass wool are self-forming and usually fit well. A professional should fit your workers individually for molded or preformed earplugs. Clean earplugs regularly, and replace those you cannot clean.

Protection from Hand Injuries
Workers exposed to harmful substances through skin absorption, severe cuts or lacerations, severe abrasions, chemical burns, thermal burns, and harmful temperatureextremes will benefit from hand protection.

Protection from Body Injury
In some cases workers must shield most or all of their bodies against hazards in the workplace, such as exposure to heat and radiation as well as hot metals, scalding liquids, body fluids, hazardous materials or waste, and other hazards. In addition to fire-retardant wool and fireretardant cotton, materials used in whole-body personal protective equipment include rubber, leather, synthetics, and plastic.

When to Wear Respiratory Protection
When engineering controls are not feasible, workers must use appropriate respirators to protect against adverse health effects caused by breathing air contaminated with harmful dusts, fogs, fumes, mists, gases, smokes, sprays, or vapors. Respirators generally cover the nose and mouth or the entire face or head and help prevent illness and injury. A proper fit is essential, however, for respirators to be effective. Required respirators must be NIOSH-approved and medical evaluation and training must be provided before use.

Additional Information
For additional information concerning protective equipment view the publication, Assessing the Need for Personal Protective Equipment: A Guide for Small Business Employers (OSHA 3151) available on OSHA's web site at www. osha. gov. For more information about personal protective equipment in the construction industry, visit www.osha-slc.gov/SLTC/construc-tionppe/ index.html.

Contacting OSHA
To report an emergency, file a complaint or seek OSHA advice, assistance or products, call (800) 321-OSHA or contact your nearest OSHA regional or area office.

This is one in a series of informational fact sheets highlighting OSHA programs, policies or standards. It does not impose any new compliance requirements. For a comprehensive list of compliance requirements of OSHA standards or regulations, refer to Title 29 of the Code of Federal Regulations. This information will be made available to sensory impaired individuals upon request. The voice phone is (202) 693-1999; teletypewriter (TTY) number: (877) 889-5627.

For more complete information:

OSHA® Occupational Safety and Health Administration

U.S. Department of Labor
www.osha.gov
(800) 321-OSHA

DOC 4/2006

Name: _____   Date: _____

Knowledge Check: PPE

1. Who is responsible for providing PPE?
    a. The employer
    b. The employee
    c. OSHA
    d. Workers' Compensation

2. Common causes of foot injuries include: crushing, penetration, molten metal, chemicals, slippery surfaces, and sharp objects.
    a. True
    b. False

3. Safety controls must meet the following order of priority:
    a. Substitution, PPE, workaround, and administrative
    b. Workaround, stop work, PPE, and engineering
    c. Stop work, PPE, engineering, and substitution
    d. Substitution, engineering, administrative, and PPE

4. Which type of hard hat would provide the most protection from electrical hazards?
    a. Class A
    b. Class C
    c. Class E
    d. Class G

5. The need for hearing protection is triggered at which decibel level?
    a. When it exceeds 80 decibels
    b. When it exceeds 90 decibels
    c. When it exceeds 100 decibels
    d. When it exceeds 110 decibels

6. Who is responsible for providing specialized work footwear?
    a. The employer
    b. The employee
    c. OSHA
    d. Insurance companies

7. Which of the following is considered approved eye protection?
    a. Sun glasses
    b. Prescription glasses
    c. Reading glasses
    d. Glasses meeting ANSI standard Z87

8. Which of the following is not considered PPE?
    a. Rubber gloves
    b. Glasses meeting ANSI Z87
    c. Sports shoes
    d. Hearing muffs

Focus 4: Falls

Guardrail and Safety Net Systems Summary

Guardrail and safety net systems are two ways to protect workers from falls on the job. If you are more than 6 feet above the lower surface, some type of fall protection must be used by your employer.

If your employer uses **guardrails:**

- Toprails must be at least ¼ inch thick to prevent cuts and lacerations; and they must be between 39 and 45 inches from the working surface;
- If wire rope is used, it must be flagged at least every six feet with highly visible materials;
- Midrails, screens or mesh must be installed when there are no walls at least 21 inches high. Screens and mesh must extend from the toprail to the working level.
- There can be no openings more than 19 inches;
- The toprail must withstand at least 200 lbs. of force; the midrail must withstand 150 lbs. of force;
- The system must be smooth enough to protect workers from cuts and getting their clothes snagged by the rail.
- If guardrails are used around holes at points of access, like a ladderway, a gate must be used to prevent someone from falling through the hole, or be offset so that a person cannot walk directly into the hole.

If your employer uses **safety nets**:

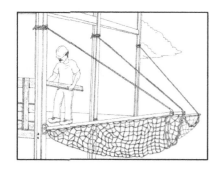

- The nets must be as close as practicable under the working surface, but never more than 30 feet below;
- The safety net must be inspected every week for damage;
- Each net must have a border rope with a minimum strength of 5,000 lbs.;
- The safety net must extend outward a sufficient distance, depending on how far the net is from the working surface (OSHA has a formula to follow);
- The safety net must absorb the force of a 400-pound bag of sand dropping on to the net ("the drop test");
- Items in the net that could be dangerous must be removed as soon as possible.

Personal Fall Arrest Systems Summary

Personal fall arrest systems are one way to protect workers from falls. In general, workers must have fall protection when they could fall 6 feet or more while they are working.

OSHA **requires** workers to wear a full-body harness, (one part of a *Personal Fall Arrest System*) when they are working on a *suspended scaffold* more than *10 feet* above the working surface, or when they are working in *bucket truck or aerial lift*. Employers may also choose to use a Personal Fall Arrest System, instead of a guardrail, when workers are working on a *supported scaffold* more than 10 feet above the working surface.

There are **three** major components of a Personal Fall Arrest System (PFAS):

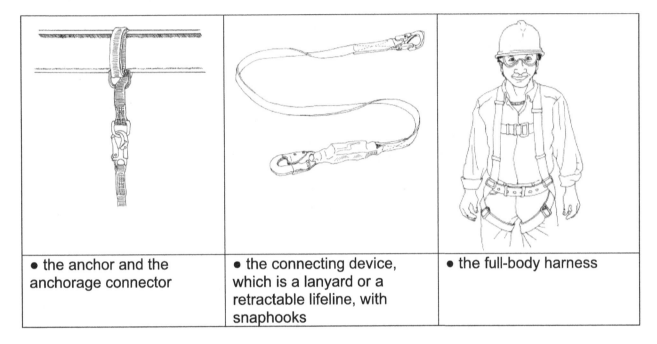

• the anchor and the anchorage connector	• the connecting device, which is a lanyard or a retractable lifeline, with snaphooks	• the full-body harness

The following are some things to remember about personal fall arrest systems:

1. A personal fall arrest system is made up of an **anchorage, connecting device, and a full-body harness**. The connecting device may be a lanyard with snaphooks, or a self-retracting lifeline. A lanyard could also include a deceleration device. Make sure you are using components from the same manufacturer to ensure that the system works as it should. If not, any substitution or change must be evaluated or tested by a competent person to ensure that it meets the standard.

2. **Body belts cannot be used** for fall arresting service. However, a body belt is allowed as part of a positioning system. A positioning system is one way to prevent falls from occurring. It involves equipment for keeping your body in a position where you are not able to fall. For all situations where you could actually fall, you need to wear a full-body harness.

3. Your personal fall arrest system must be **inspected for damage** each time before you wear it. [If there are defects, or if someone has taken a fall using the equipment, it must be removed from service.]

4. The **attachment location** of the body harness must be in the center of your back, near the shoulder level or above your head.

5. **Vertical lifelines or lanyards** must have a minimum breaking strength of 5,000 lbs., and be protected against being cut or abraded.

6. Each worker must be attached to a **separate vertical lifeline**. [There is a special exception when constructing elevator shafts.]

7. The **webbing**, which is the materials used for ropes and straps of lifelines, lanyard and harnesses, must be made of **synthetic** fibers.

8. **An anchorage** for workers' personal fall arrest equipment must be **independent of any anchorage** used to support or suspend platforms, and it must be able to support at least 5,000 lbs. per worker attached to it.

9. **Connectors** must be made from **steel or equivalent** materials, with a corrosion-resistant finish and the edges must be smooth.

10. **D-rings and snaphooks** must have a **minimum tensile strength** of 5,000 lbs.

11. **Snaphooks** must be a **locking-type** (they are generally double-locking) and designed to prevent the snaphook from opening and slipping off the connector.

12. **Snaphooks cannot be *directly connected*** to the webbing, rope or wire, to each other, to a D-ring to which another snaphook or other connector is attached, to a horizontal lifeline, or to any other object that could cause the snaphook to open.

Preventing Ladder Falls - *Construction Safety*

Why construction falls?

Here area few basic facts about falls in construction:
-- Every day, four construction workers die on the job.
-- Falls are the most common cause of fatal injuries to construction workers.
-- The consequences of a fall affect not only the worker, but also his or her family and community.

-- Construction falls can be prevented. Contractors and foreman can do many things to organize the worksite to be safer for their employees. But workers themselves can also make some inexpensive, simple changes to the way they work that can save their lives.
-- Ladders are one of the most common pieces of equipment on a construction site. But that doesn't mean they are safe. There are construction workers who are injured or killed falling from a height every day. Using ladders more safely is one way to start preventing falls at your work site.

Set an example at work

Your co-workers can learn a lot from you. At first, you might be the only one who is concerned with safety at your worksite. But over time, other workers will see that the foreman will give you the time you need to be safe. They will see how many little things add up to big effects on safety. And they will see how they, too, can help to make your worksite safer.

So, set an example. Don't worry about being the first—they'll thank you for it later.

How can I prevent a fall from a ladder?

There are many ways you can prevent a fall from a ladder—here are just three suggestions to get you started.

- Choose the right ladder for the job.
- Tie the top and bottom of the ladder to fixed points when necessary.
- Don't carry tools or other materials in-hand while climbing the ladder.

1. Choose the right ladder for the job.

- First you need to make sure that a ladder is the best equipment for what you need to do. Would scaffolding or a mechanical lift be better?
- Many times, the ladder is the only physical support you have while you are working. If it fails, you can fall. That's why it is so important to find the right ladder when you do need to use one. The three main types of ladders—step ladders, straight ladders, and extension ladders—are used in different situations for different tasks.
- Before you start using a ladder, ask yourself two questions.
- **Is the ladder long enough?** It should be long enough for you to set it at a stable angle and still extend at the top to give you something to hold on to when you get

on the ladder to descend. Setting the ladder at the right angle helps you keep your balance on the ladder. It also helps keep the ladder from falling backwards.

- Make sure the ladder extends 3 feet (3 rungs; 0.9 meters) above the surface you will be working on.
- Make sure the ladder is placed at a stable angle. For every four feet (1.2 m) high the ladder is, the base should be 1 foot (.3 m) out from the wall
- For example, if you will be working on a 10 foot-high roof (3 m), you need a ladder that is at least 14 feet (4.25 m) long. The base should be 2 ½ feet (.75 m) from the wall.
- **Is the ladder in good working condition?** It shouldn't be missing pieces or be cracked or otherwise damaged. Check the duty rating on extension ladders – is it high enough for the weight you will be putting on it? Longer ladders don't always have higher duty ratings, so be sure to check. In construction, the most common ratings are:
  - Heavy Duty (I) supports up to 250 pounds (113 kg).
  - Extra heavy duty (IA) supports up to 300 pounds (136 kg).
  - Special duty (IAA) supports up to 375 pounds (170 kg).

2. Tie the top and bottom of the ladder to fixed points when necessary: if it doesn't extend 3' above the landing, on slippery surfaces, and where it could be displaced by work activities or traffic.

- Tie both sides of the top of the ladder to a fixed point on the roof or other high surface near where you are working. The bottom should be tied to a fixed point on the ground. Securing the ladder in this way prevents the ladder from sliding side-to-side or falling backwards and prevents the base from sliding.
- Tying the ladder off at the beginning of the day and untying it at the end will only take you about 5 minutes. It can make all the difference for your safety. If you need to move the ladder around, allow extra time for this important step, or consider using something else, such as a scaffold.

3. Don't carry tools or other materials in-hand while climbing the ladder.

- Take precautions when you are going up or down a ladder. Instead of carrying tools, boards, or other materials in your hands, use a tool belt, install a rope and pulley system, or tie a rope around your materials and pull them up once you have reached the work surface. Ask for help if you need to use more than one hand to pull them up.
- Carrying tools or anything else in your hands as you climb the ladder can throw you off balance. When you climb a ladder, always use at least one hand to grasp the ladder when going up or down.

Scaffold Work Can Be Dangerous: Know the Basics of Scaffold Safety

There are thousands of scaffold-related injuries – and about 40 scaffold-related deaths – every year in the U.S. If you are doing work on scaffolds, know how to work on them safely – it could save your life!

Here are some rules about scaffolds that must be followed if you want to work safely:

1. A **competent person** must be available to direct workers who are constructing or moving scaffolds. The competent person must also train workers, and **inspect** the scaffold and its components **before every work shift, and after any event that could affect the structural integrity of the scaffold**. The competent person must be able to identify unsafe conditions, and be authorized by the employer to take action to correct unsafe conditions, to make the workplace safe. And a **qualified person**, someone who has very specific knowledge or training, must actually design the scaffold and its rigging.

2. Every **supported** scaffold and its components must **support, without failure, its own weight and at least four times the intended load**. The intended load is the sum of the weights of all personnel, tools and materials that will be placed on the scaffold. Don't load the scaffold with more weight than it can safely handle.

3. On **supported** scaffolds, working platforms/decks must be planked close to the guardrails. Planks are to be overlapped on a support at least 6 inches, but not more than 12 inches.

4. Inspections of **supported** scaffolds must include:
   - Checking metal components for bends, cracks, holes, rust, welding splatter, pits, broken welds and non-compatible parts.
   - Covering and securing floor openings and labeling floor opening covers.

5. Each rope on a **suspended** scaffold must support the scaffold's weight and at least **six times** the intended load.

6. Scaffold **platforms** must be at least **18 inches wide, (there are some exceptions),** and guardrails and/or personal fall arrest systems must be used for fall protection any time you are working 10 feet or more above ground level. **Guardrails** must be between 39 and 45 inches high, and **midrails** must be installed approximately halfway between the toprail and the platform surface.

7. OSHA standards require that workers have **fall protection when working on a scaffold 10 or more feet above the ground**. OSHA requires the following:

- The use of a **guardrail OR** a **personal fall arrest system** when working on a *supported scaffold*.
- **BOTH** a guardrail **AND** a **personal fall arrest system** when working on a *single-point or two-point suspended scaffold*.
- A **personal fall arrest system** when working on an *aerial lift*.

8. Your lifeline must be tied back to **a structural anchorage** capable of withstanding **5,000 lbs** of dead weight **per person** tied off to it. Attaching your lifeline to a guardrail, a standpipe or other piping systems will not meet the 5,000 lbs requirement and is not a safe move.

9. Wear hard hats, and make sure there are toeboards, screens and debris nets in place **to protect other people from falling objects**.

10. **Counterweights** for *suspended scaffolds* must be able to resist at least **four times the *tipping moment***, and they must be made of materials that cannot be easily dislocated (no sand, no water, no rolls of roofing, etc.). [This would be calculated by the *qualified person* who designs the scaffold.]

11. Your employer must provide safe access to the scaffold when a platform is more than two (2) feet above or below the point of access, or when you need to step across more than 14 inches to get on the platform. **Climbing on cross braces is not allowed!** Ladders, stair towers, ramps and walkways are some of the ways of providing safe access.

12. All workers must be **trained** on:
   o how to use the scaffold, and how to recognize hazards associated with the type of scaffold they are working on;
   o the maximum intended load and capacity;
   o how to recognize and report defects;
   o fall hazards, falling object hazards and any other hazards that may be encountered, including electrical hazards (such as overhead power lines); and,
   o having proper fall protection systems in place.

Read the following scenario; ask participants to take on the roles of Mike, Joe and the foreman. After reading the story, participants should identify all the **wrong** things that the workers did when working with ladders; discuss the RIGHT way to work safely on a ladder.

Roles: Mike and Joe, the workers and Mr. Smith, the foreman

INTRODUCTION:

Joe and Mike are excited; they just got the call to work on the new residential construction project in the area. They don't have much experience, but the pay is good, and they want to use this job as a stepping stone to bigger and better jobs. It's their first day on the job.

SCENE ONE: The foreman's office

Mr. Smith: So you know how to work on ladders, right guys?

Joe: Well, I haven't had a lot of experience, so maybe you could just go over the basics…

Mr. Smith: Well, I have to take this delivery, and I thought you told me you had lots of experience – where was your last job, anyway? We've got a deadline on this project, so….

Mike: Don't worry, Mr. Smith, I'll explain it all to him. I used ladders a lot on my last job.

Unsafe Work:
"What's wrong with this picture?"

Mr. Smith: Okay. First you need to paint the trim around the top of the building, and then, go inside and finish with the painting in the lobby. There are a couple of extension ladders out here, and a couple of step ladders inside. One of you should work out here, and the other start inside. Are you sure you know what to do? I asked them to find me some experienced guys, not rookies…

Mike: We're fine, Mr. Smith. We'll call you if we have any questions.

LADDER SAFETY: What's Wrong with this Picture?

SCENE TWO: Mike and Joe are outside setting up.
Mike: So Joe, you work out here, and I'll do the inside work, okay?

Joe: Sure, but can you help me to set up here? Is this extension ladder okay, and how do I set it up?

Mike: Well, first you should inspect it. Of course the ladder needs to be long enough to reach the top, and it has to be able to hold you. So check the information on the ladder. It says it's a Type I – I'm not sure what that means, but I think it has something to do with your weight. How heavy are you?

Joe: About 260 pounds – I've been eating like a horse lately. I have to get back to the gym.

Mike: Well, that should be good enough. And how long is the ladder, and how high to the roof?

Joe: It says it's a 24-foot ladder, and the building is about 20 feet tall.

Mike: Okay, that should work. Just be careful if you're climbing onto the roof.

Joe: Am I supposed to check the ladder before using it?

Mike: Yeah, but this one looks fine to me.

Joe: Well, the step pads are ripped, and there is no pad on one of the feet – won't that make it uneven?

Mike: Just wrap some of this tape around it to even it off. I don't want to be asking for too much on our first day, you know?

Unsafe Work:
"What's wrong with this picture?"

Joe: This bolt seems a bit loose, and the pulley rope is a bit frayed. I wonder how that happened…and the steps feel like they have some kind of slippery stuff on them…

Mike: So just wipe them off. Listen, we need to get started here…

Joe: Okay, okay, let's just set up then. Where should I start?

LADDER SAFETY: What's Wrong with this Picture?

Mike: Start over by the doorway; it's early in the day, so not many people should be walking in and out. If you see anyone, just yell. And it's windy already, and it's supposed to get worse later on, so be careful.

Joe: Okay. The ground is pretty uneven here with all these rocks. And do I need to worry about those electrical wires? They seem like they are pretty close to the ladder.

Mike: Man, you ask a lot of questions, dude! Let's get this set up. Okay, you need to set this up at the right angle to make sure you don't fall. I remember that the ratio is 1 foot of length from the wall for every...every 5 feet of height, I think. So the building is 20 feet high, so put the ladder 4 feet from the wall.

Joe: That seems a little steep, doesn't it?

Mike: No, that's right. And remember that if we do well on this job, we get another one with this company, so we need to move fast. I will be inside, so don't keep calling me to help you. Carry the paint up with you – try to bring up a couple of cans the first time up to save time.

Joe: Should I try to tie the ladder to something so it doesn't move?

Mike: Don't worry about it moving at the top; just use this rope to tie the ladder to this bicycle stand.

Joe: And who left all these cans and plants around? Someone is going to trip on this stuff!

Mike: Yeah, yeah, don't worry about it; someone may be looking to use the stuff, so leave it there for now. I'm going inside to start on the lobby; I'll take one of these step ladders. See you later.

Joe: Yeah, see you.

Unsafe Work:
"What's wrong with this picture both inside and outside?

LADDER SAFETY: What's Wrong with this Picture?

SCENE THREE: Mike is inside, using the step ladder.

Mr. Smith: Hey Mike, how's it going?

Mike: Great, Mr. Smith, this is a great job.

Mr. Smith: Be careful, you should not be sitting on the ladder, and before I saw you standing on the top step.

Mike: Oh, don't worry, Mr. Smith, I can handle myself on a ladder – I've been working with my father for years doing this kind of work.

Mr. Smith: Okay, but try not to lean so far; just get down and walk the ladder closer, okay?

Mike: No problem, Mr. Smith, I'm a good worker, and I work fast. Suddenly, they hear Joe yelling from outside, and then they hear a "thud." They run outside to see what happened.

LADDER SAFETY: What's Wrong with this Picture?

Consider the Ladder Safety scenario to complete this worksheet.

1. Are there any problems with Joe's and Mike's ladder work?

_____
_____
_____
_____
_____
_____
_____
_____
_____
_____
_____
_____
_____
_____

2. What could have been the reason for Joe's fall?

_____
_____
_____
_____
_____
_____
_____
_____
_____
_____
_____
_____
_____

3. Do you think Mike is working safely? Why or why not?

_____
_____
_____
_____
_____
_____
_____
_____
_____
_____
_____
_____
_____

Personal Fall Arrest System Checklist

Personal Fall Arrest Systems are one way to protect workers on construction sites where there are vertical drops of 6 or more feet. Systems must be set up so that a worker cannot fall more than 6 feet, nor come into contact with any lower level.

You should be able to answer **Yes** to each of the following.

1. Is your Personal Fall Arrest System made up of an anchorage, connecting device, and a full-body harness?

2. Are the components from the same manufacturer to ensure that the system works as it should? If not, has any substitution or change to a personal fall arrest system been fully evaluated or tested by a competent person to determine that it meets the standard?

3. Has your personal fall arrest system been inspected for damage each time before you wear it? [If there are defects, or if someone has taken a fall using the equipment, it must be removed from service.]

4. Is the attachment location of the body harness in the center of your back, near the shoulder level or above your head?

5. Do vertical lifelines or lanyards have a minimum breaking strength of 5,000 lbs? Are they protected against being cut or abraded?

6. Will each worker be attached to a separate vertical lifeline?

7. Is the webbing, [the materials used for ropes and straps of lifelines, lanyard and harnesses] made of synthetic fibers?

8. Is the anchorage for workers' personal fall arrest equipment independent of any anchorage used to support or suspend platforms? Is it able to support at least 5,000 lbs. per worker attached to it?

9. Are the connectors made from steel or equivalent materials, with a corrosion-resistant finish and smooth edges?

10. Do the D-rings and snaphooks have a minimum tensile strength of 5,000 lbs.?

11. Are snaphooks of a locking-type and designed to prevent the snaphook from opening and slipping off the connector?

12. Are the snaphooks not *directly connected* to the webbing, rope or wire, to each other, to a D-ring to which another snaphook or other connector is attached, to a horizontal lifeline, or to any other object that could cause the snaphook to open?

Fall Hazard Recognition
Student Copy
Take notes and record the details of the hazards that may be present

Is This a Fall Hazard?

Photos in this presentation are from the OSHA Region 4 National Photo Archive and OSHA Region 5.

1

_____

_____

_____

_____

_____

_____

_____

Any Fall Hazard Here?

3

_____

_____

_____

_____

_____

_____

_____

Is This a Fall Hazard?

5

_____

_____

_____

_____

_____

_____

_____

Any Fall Hazard Here?

7

Is This a Fall Hazard?

9

Can You Identify the Fall Hazard?

11

Can You Identify the Fall Hazard?

13

_____

_____

_____

_____

_____

_____

_____

Is This a Fall Hazard?

15

_____

_____

_____

_____

_____

_____

_____

Can You Identify the Fall Hazards?

17

_____

_____

_____

_____

_____

_____

_____

Any Fall Hazard Here?

19

Is This a Fall Hazard?

21

Is This a Fall Hazard?

23

Name: _____   Date: _____

1. In general, fall protection must be provided to construction workers who are working on surfaces with unprotected sides and edges which are _____ above the lower level:
   a. 3 feet
   b. 4 feet
   c. 6 feet

2. What are the ways an employer can protect workers from falls?
   a. Guardrails, safety net systems and safety belts
   b. Guardrails and safety nets
   c. Guardrails, safety net systems and personal fall arrest systems

3. For workers on scaffolds, fall protection must be provided if they are working _____ above a lower level.
   a. 4 feet
   b. 6 feet
   c. 10 feet

4. Guardrails are often used by employers to protect workers from falls. How high must the top guardrail (the toprail) be above the working surface?
   a. 24 inches, plus or minus 3 inches
   b. 42 inches, plus or minus 3 inches
   c. 60 inches, plus or minus 3 inches

5. A personal fall arrest system consists of:
   a. An anchorage and a body belt
   b. An anchorage, lanyard and connectors, and a body belt
   c. An anchorage, lanyard and connectors, and a full body harness

6. The top of a ladder must extend at least _____ above the surface you are climbing onto.
   a. 3 feet
   b. 4 feet
   c. 5 feet

Focus 4: Electrocution

General Rules for Construction

Electrical Safety

MAJOR PROTECTIVE METHODS FROM ELECTRICAL HAZARDS

Protection from electrical hazards generally includes the following methods:

1. **DISTANCE**: Commonly used with regard to power lines.

2. **ISOLATION AND GUARDING**: Restricting access, commonly used with high voltage power distribution equipment.

3. **ENCLOSURE OF ELECTRICAL PARTS**: A major concept of electrical wiring in general, e.g. all connections are made in a box.

4. **GROUNDING**: Required for all non-current carrying exposed metal parts, unless isolated or guarded as above. (However, corded tools may be either *grounded* OR be *double-insulated*.)

5. **INSULATION**: Intact insulation allows safe handling of everyday electrical equipment, including of everyday electrical equipment, including corded tools. Category also includes insulated mats and sleeves.

6. **DE-ENERGIZING AND GROUNDING**: Protective method used by electrical utilities and also in conjunction with electrical lockout/tagout.

7. **PERSONAL PROTECTIVE EQUIPMENT (PPE)**: Using insulated gloves and other apparel to work on energized equipment, limited to qualified and trained personnel working under very limited circumstances.

Effects of Electric Current in the Human Body

Current / Reaction
(1,000 milliamperes = 1 amp; therefore, 15,000 milliamperes = 15 amp circuit)
Below 1 milliampere Generally not perceptible
1 milliampere Faint tingle
5 milliampere Slight shock felt; not painful but disturbing. Average individual can let go. Strong involuntary reactions can lead to other injuries.
6-25 milliamperes (women) Painful shock, loss of muscular control
9-30 milliamperes (men) The freezing current or "let-go" range. Individual cannot let go, but can be thrown away from the circuit if extensor muscles are stimulated.
50-150 milliamperes Extreme pain, respiratory arrest, severe muscular contractions. Death is possible.
1,000 - 4,300 milliamperes Rhythmic pumping action of the heart ceases. Muscular contraction and nerve damage occur; death likely.
10,000 milliamperes Cardiac arrest, severe burns; death probable

OSHA®

Construction Focus Four: Electrocution
Directorate of Training and Education
2020 S. Arlington Heights Rd
Arlington Heights, IL 60005

Some content adapted from: Central New York COSH 2007, Construction Safety & Health Electrocution hazards Grantee module, Grant Number SH-16586-07-06-F-36 from OSHA

www.osha.gov

Construction Focus Four: Electrocution

Safety Tips for Workers

Contents:

- Electrical Safety Overview
- General Rules for Electrical Work
- Condensed Electrical Glossary
- General Rules for Construction
- Electrical Safety
- Effects of Electric Current in the Human Body

Electrical Safety Overview

1 CORD AND PLUG OPERATED electric tools with exposed metal parts must have a three-prong grounding plug – AND be grounded – or else be double-insulated.

2 EQUIPMENT GROUNDING only works when there is a permanent and continuous electrical connection between the metal shell of a tool and the earth.

3 PROPER POLARITY IN ELECTRICAL WIRING IS IMPORTANT: hot to hot, neutral to neutral equipment ground to equipment ground. Polarized plugs have a wider neutral blade to maintain correct polarity. *Reversed polarity can kill.*

4 CIRCUITS MUST BE EQUIPPED WITH FUSES OR CIRCUIT BREAKERS to protect against dangerous overloads. *Fuses melt, while circuit breakers trip to turn off currents like a switch. Overcurrent protection devices protect wiring and equipment from overheating and fires. They may, or may not protect you.*

5 MOST 120 VOLT CIRCUITS are wired to deliver up to 15 or 20 amps of current. Currents of 50 – 100 milliamperes can kill you. *(1 mA = 1/1,000 of 1 Amp)*

6 WET CONDITIONS LOWER SKIN RESISTANCE, allowing more current to flow through your body. *Currents above 75 milliamps can cause ventricular fibrillation, which may be fatal. Severity of a shock depends on: path of current, amount of current, duration of current, voltage level, moisture and your general health.*

7 A GROUND FAULT CIRCUIT INTERRUPTER (GFCI) protects from a ground-fault, the most common electrical hazard GFCIs detect differences in current flow between hot and neutral. They trip when there is current leakage – such as through a person – of about 5 milliamperes and they act within 1/40 of a second. Test a GFCI every time you use it. It must "Trip" and it must "Reset."

8 EXTENSION CORD WIRES MUST BE HEAVY ENOUGH for the amount of current they will carry. For construction, they must be UL approved, have strain relief and a 3-prong grounding plug, be durable, and be rated for hard or extra-hard usage.

9 OVERHEAD POWER LINES CAN KILL. The three major methods of protection are: maintaining a safe distance, de-energizing AND grounding lines, having the power company install insulating sleeves. Have a power company rep on the site.

10 UNDERGROUND POWER LINES CAN KILL. Call before you dig to locate all underground cables. Hand dig within three feet of cable location!

General Rules for Electrical Work

- *Non-conductive PPE is essential for electricians. NO METAL PPE! Class B hard hats provide the highest level of protection against electrical hazards, with high-voltage shock and burn protection (up to 20,000 volts). Electrical hazard, safety-toe shoes are nonconductive and will prevent the wearer's feet from completing an electrical circuit to the ground.*

- Be alert to electrical hazards, especially when working with ladders, scaffolds and other platforms.

- Never bypass electrical protective systems or devices.

- Disconnect cord tools when not in use and when changing blades, bits or other accessories.

- Inspect all tools before use.

- Use only grounded extension cords.

- Remove damaged tools and damaged extension cords from use.

- Keep working spaces and walkways clear of electrical cords.

RULES FOR TEMPORARY WIRING AND LIGHTING

- Use Ground Fault Circuit Interrupters (GFCIs) on all 15-Amp and 20-Amp temporary wiring circuits.

- Protect temporary lights from contact and damage.

- Don't suspend temporary lights by cords, unless the temporary light is so designed

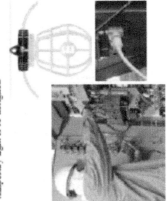

Condensed Electrical Glossary

AMPERE OR AMP: The unit of electrical current (flow of electrons). ● One milliamp (mA) = 1/1,000 of 1 Amp.

CONDUCTORS: Materials, such as metals, in which electrical current can flow.

ELECTRICAL HAZARDS can result in various effects on the body, including: ● **SHOCK** – The physical effects caused by electric current flowing in the body. ● **ELECTROCUTION** – Electrical shock or related electrical effects resulting in death ● **BURNS** – Often occurring on the hands, thermal damage to tissue can be caused by the flow of current in the body, by overheating of improper or damaged electrical component, or by an arc flash. ● **FALLS** – A common effect, sometimes caused by the body's reaction to an electrical current. A non-fatal shock may sometimes result in a fatal fall when a person is working on an elevated surface.

EXPOSED LIVE PARTS: Energized electrical components not properly enclosed in a box or otherwise isolated, such that workers can touch them and be shocked or killed. Some of the common hazards include: missing knock-outs, unused openings in cabinets and missing covers. Covers must not be removed from wiring or breaker boxes. Any missing covers must be replaced with approved covers.

INSULATORS: Materials with high electrical resistance, so electrical current can't flow.

LOCKOUT/TAGOUT: The common name for an OSHA standard. *"The control of hazardous energy (lockout tagout) Lockout is a means of controlling energy during repair and maintenance of equipment, whereby energy sources are de-energized, isolated and then locked out to prevent unsafe startup of equipment which would endanger workers. Lockout includes - but is not limited to - the control of electrical energy. Tagout means the placing of warning tags to alert other workers to the presence of equipment that has been locked out. Tags alone DO NOT LOCK OUT equipment. Tagout is most effective when done in addition to lockout.*

OHM or Ω: The unit of electrical resistance (opposition to current flow).

OHM'S LAW: A mathematical expression of the relationship among voltage (volts), current (amps) and resistance (ohm). This is often expressed as: $E = I \times R$. In this case, E = volts, I = amp and R = ohms. (The equation, Amps = Volts/Ohms, is used in this curriculum, is one form of Ohm's Law)

VOLT: The unit of electromotive force (emf) caused by a difference in electrical charge or electrical potential between one point and another point. The presence of voltage is necessary before current can flow in a circuit (in which current flows from a source to a load – the equipment using the electricity and then back to its source).

WET CONDITIONS: Rain, sweat, standing in a puddle – all will decrease the skin's electrical resistance and increase current flow through the body in the event of a shock. Have a qualified electrician inspect any electrical equipment that has gotten wet before energizing it.

Focus Four [Electrocution] Toolbox Talks 1:

What increases your risk of electrocution?

[Ask the following questions and give time for answers.]

What are the hazards? Bodily contact with electricity

What are the results? Shock, fire, burns, falls or death

What should we look for? Damaged equipment, faulty wiring, improper cord use, no GFCIs, wet conditions, reverse polarity, potential arc flash areas, lack of assured equipment grounding conductor program

[Relate this incident or, better, one you know.]

Actual Incident: A 40-year-old male plumber died after lying on his work light while installing plumbing under a house being remodeled. The victim was crawling under the house carrying the work light with him. The wire inside the work light's conduit became bare and energized the light's housing. Investigation of the incident showed a damaged work light was used with no GFCI. Also, the home's electrical system was not properly grounded.

[Ask the following question and ensure every item is covered.]

How do we prevent these results?

    □ Inspect all electrical equipment before use.

    □ Use GFCI with all power tools.

    □ Use intact and properly rated cords (i.e. correct AWG).

    □ Do not use damaged equipment - take it out of service.

    □ Institute an assured equipment grounding conductor program.

    □ Do not work in wet conditions with electricity.

[Ask the following questions about this site and ensure every item is covered.]

Let's talk about this site now.

    □ What factors increase your chance of being electrocuted?

    □ Can someone demonstrate how to inspect this tool for electrical safety? (If possible, provide a tool)

    □ What are some areas on the site that could use attention pertaining to electrical hazards?

What are the hazards show in these photos?

[Record questions below that you want to ask about this site.]

Focus Four [Electrocution] Toolbox Talks 2:

What protective devices and procedures can you use to prevent electrocution?

[Ask the following questions and give time for answers.]

What are the hazards? Bodily contact with electricity due to faulty equipment, ungrounded or damaged equipment, wet conditions, etc.

What are the results? Shock, fire, burns, falls or death

What should we look for? Proper training in using engineering controls (e.g. GFCIs, proper cords), assured equipment grounding conductor written program, electrical testing meters

[Relate this incident or, better, one you know.]

Actual Incident: A 29-year- old male welder was electrocuted and died when he contacted an energized receptacle end of an extension cord. It was found that the welding unit and cord were incompatible; however, both the welding cord and extension cord were damaged allowing them to be used together. The result was an ungrounded system that killed a worker.

American Wire Gauge (AWG)	
Cord Size	Handles Up To
#10 AWG	30 amps
#12 AWG	25 amps
#14 AWG	18 amps
#16 AWG	13 amps

[Ask the following question and ensure every item is covered.]

How do we prevent these results?

- Inspect all electrical equipment before use.
- Use GFCI with all power tools.
- Use intact and properly-rated cords (i.e. correct AWG).
- Do not use damaged equipment - take it out of service.
- Institute an assured equipment grounding conductor program.
- Use testing meters, where appropriate, if you are trained to do so.

[Ask the following questions about this site and ensure every item is covered.]

Let's talk about this site now.

- Can someone explain how a GFCI works? (If possible, provide a GFCI to use).
- Who has read this site's assured equipment grounding conductor program?
- What are some of the requirements?

[Record questions below that you want to ask about this site.]

Focus Four [Electrocution] Toolbox Talks 3:

How can we prevent electrocutions while using power tools?

[Ask the following questions and give time for answers.]

What are the hazards? Bodily contact with electricity

What are the results? Shock, fire, burns, falls or death

What should we look for? Tools that aren't double-insulated, damaged tools and cords, incorrect cords, wet conditions, tools used improperly

[Relate this incident or, better, one you know.]

Actual Incident: A 45-year-old male electrician was electrocuted when he contacted an energized 1/2" electric drill casing. The victim was working in wet conditions and using a single insulated drill attached to damaged extensions cords run through water.

[Ask the following question and ensure every item is covered.]

How do we prevent these results?

- ❑ Get proper training on manufacturers' tool use and specs.
- ❑ Inspect tool before each use according to manufacturers' instructions.
- ❑ Do not use damaged tools, remove them from service.
- ❑ Use only battery-powered tools in wet conditions.
- ❑ Use with GFCI.
- ❑ Use with properly sized and intact cords.

[Ask the following questions about this site and ensure every item is covered.]

Let's talk about this site now.

- ❑ What can lead to an electrocution while using power tools? *Non double-insulated tools, damaged cord, wet conditions*
- ❑ Have you seen or used any defective power tool?
- ❑ What should you do if you find a defective power tool?

[Record questions below that you want to ask about this site.]

Electrical Safety

Electrical hazards can cause burns, shocks and electrocution (death).

Safety Tips

- Assume that all overhead wires are energized at lethal voltages. Never assume that a wire is safe to touch even if it is down or appears to be insulated.

- Never touch a fallen overhead power line. Call the electric utility company to report fallen electrical lines.

- Stay at least 10 feet (3 meters) away from overhead wires during cleanup and other activities. If working at heights or handling long objects, survey the area before starting work for the presence of overhead wires.

- If an overhead wire falls across your vehicle while you are driving, stay inside the vehicle and continue to drive away from the line. If the engine stalls, do not leave your vehicle. Warn people not to touch the vehicle or the wire. Call or ask someone to call the local electric utility company and emergency services.

- Never operate electrical equipment while you are standing in water.

- Never repair electrical cords or equipment unless qualified and authorized.

- Have a qualified electrician inspect electrical equipment that has gotten wet before energizing it.

- If working in damp locations, inspect electric cords and equipment to ensure that they are in good condition and free of defects, and use a ground-fault circuit interrupter (GFCI).

- Always use caution when working near electricity.

For more complete information:

OSHA Occupational
Safety and Health
Administration
U.S. Department of Labor
www.osha.gov   (800) 321-OSHA

OSHA 3294-08R 09

47

Source: Central New York (COSH) Susan Harwood Training Grant #SH-16586-07-06-F-36

In your small group, read fact sheets A1 and A2, and the following scenario. Then answer the questions that follow.

- You're an experienced worker in building maintenance, helping a new worker to learn the job. The task involves cleaning up a flooded basement. The new worker has started setting up electrical cords and tools for the job. You tell her, "Hold on a minute, let's check out the wiring first." Then you say, "No, we can't do this without GFCI protection. I'll tell you why."

1. What would you tell your new co-worker?

_____
_____
_____
_____
_____
_____
_____
_____

2. What can you do to correct this problem for now?

_____
_____
_____
_____
_____
_____
_____
_____
_____
_____

3. What is the best way to deal with this in the future?

_____
_____
_____
_____
_____
_____
_____
_____
_____

4. What work practices help protect you against electrical hazards?

_____
_____
_____
_____
_____
_____
_____
_____
_____
_____
_____
_____

Examples of accidents related to wet conditions/ground fault circuit interrupters

A journeyman HVAC worker was installing metal duct work using a double-insulated drill connected to a drop light cord. Power was supplied through two extension cords from a nearby residence. The individual's perspiration-soaked clothing/body contacted bare exposed conductors on one of the cords, causing an electrocution. No GFCI's were used. Additionally, the ground prongs were missing from the two cords.

Factsheet A1 – Using Electrical Equipment in Wet Locations

Using electrical tools or equipment in wet areas can be a hazard. If your skin is dry, it has quite a lot of _resistance_ (measured in _ohms_ or Ω). However, if your skin is wet for any reason (rain, sweat, standing in a puddle of water), the skin's electrical resistance drops dramatically. The amount of electrical **current**, in _amps,_ that flows through your body **goes up when resistance** in _ohms_ **goes down. Amps = Volts/Ohms.**

The Current in **Amps** = Voltage in **Volts** DIVIDED BY Resistance in **Ohms**.
HIGHER VOLTAGE = more current (if resistance remains the same).
LOWER RESISTANCE = more current (if voltage remains the same).
HOW MUCH CURRENT DOES IT TAKE TO KILL ME?

It doesn't take much, especially if it passes through your heart. Currents above about _75 milliamps(mA)_ can cause a condition called _ventricular fibrillation._ (A milliamp is 1/1,000 of 1 amp.) If your heart goes into fibrillation, it beats very rapidly – but it doesn't pump any blood – because it's not beating in its normal rhythm. If your blood can't carry oxygen to your brain, you'll experience brain death in 3 to 4 minutes. The way to get you back involves another electric shock, from a _defibrillator._

If your skin is wet and you get your body across 120 volts of electricity, it's very likely that you'll have a current of 100 mA or more flowing through your heart. _**Currents ABOVE 10 mA**_ can cause _muscle paralysis._ You may not be able to let go of energized tools or equipment. **_Shocks that are longer in duration are more severe._**

Electrical systems must be wired with either *fuses* or *circuit breakers.* These devices are known as *overcurrent protection* and they are rated in amps. Most common household circuits are wired for 15 amps or 20 amps. **Overcurrent protection devices protect wiring and equipment from overheating and fires.** They may – or may not – protect you from electrical shock. If the current isn't high enough, the fuse won't blow or the circuit breaker won't trip. You could be shocked or killed without ever blowing a fuse or tripping a circuit breaker.

Factsheet A2 – GFCIs to the Rescue

A great breakthrough in electrical safety came with the invention of the *ground fault circuit interrupter (GFCI).* A *ground fault* occurs when electrical current flows on a path where it's not supposed to be. Under normal conditions, current flows in a circuit, traveling from the source, through the device it operates, called the *load,* and then back to the source. [See Activity 2 for more about wiring of electrical circuits.]

Current (amps) flows out to the load from the "hot" side (which is generally at 120 volts AC) and returns on the "neutral" side (which is at zero volts). Under normal conditions, these two currents (hot and neutral) are equal. If they are not equal, because of *current leakage* (current returning on a different path than the neutral conductor), we get a ground fault. This can occur if current flows through your body and returns to the source through a path to ground. **Electricity will take ANY available path to return to its source.** We want it to return only on the neutral.

The ground fault circuit interrupter (GFCI) works by using the above principles. It measures total current on the hot side and total current on the neutral side of the circuit. They are supposed to be equal. If these two currents differ from each other by *more than 5 milliamps* (plus or minus 1 mA), the GFCI acts as a fast-acting circuit breaker and shuts off the electricity within 1/40 of 1 second. You can still feel this small amount of current, but it will quickly shut off.

GFCIs are manufactured in many forms. The most common one is the GFCI outlet. However, there are also GFCI circuit breakers, plug-in GFCI outlets and GFCI extension cords, as well as GFCIs hard-wired into devices such as hair dryers. All types have **"Test"** and **"Reset"** functions. **The GFCI must trip when you press the "Test" button. It must also energize the circuit when you press "Reset." If either test fails, you must replace the GFCI in order to be protected!**

In your small group, read fact sheets B1 and B2, and the following scenario.
Then answer the questions that follow.

SCENARIO:
You're at work one day and a co-worker starts screaming: It
looks like his saw is smoking, it smells like it's burning and his
extension cord is getting hot enough to burn his hand. You
walk over, take one look at the scene and start shaking
your head. "Well, I know what your problem is, and I'll explain
if you stop shouting," you tell him.

1. What is your explanation to the worker?

_____
_____
_____
_____
_____
_____
_____
_____
_____

2. What are some steps to deal with this issue?

_____
_____
_____
_____
_____
_____
_____
_____
_____
_____

3. What is the best way to correct the problem?

_____
_____
_____
_____
_____
_____
_____
_____
_____
_____

Factsheet B1 – Wire Size and Ampacity

In terms of conducting electrical current, size matters: the size of the electrical conductor. Take a look at the following table regarding *ampacity,* the current carrying capacity of a conductor in amps. You'll notice two things: the **amount of current** a wire can safely carry **increases** as the **diameter** (and area) of the wire increases and as the number of the **wire size decreases**. Welcome to the American Wire Gauge (AWG).

AWG Copper Wire Table

Copper Wire Size (AWG)	Diameter (mils)	Area (Circular mils)	Ampacity in free air	Ampacity as part of 3-conductor cable
14 AWG	64.1	4109	20 Amps	15 Amps
12 AWG	80.8	6529	25 Amps	20 Amps
10 AWG	101.9	10,384	40 Amps	30 Amps
8 AWG	128.5	16,512	70 Amps	50 Amps

BUT I DON'T WANT TO BE AN ENGINEER...

Hey, neither do I, but this stuff is important. Notice that a #8 wire is *twice the diameter,* but *four times the area* of a #14 wire. There are a couple of practical applications here. For one thing, the gauge of the wire determines the rating of a fuse or circuit breaker in amps. A circuit wired with #14 copper will get a 15 amp circuit breaker. A circuit with #12 copper can get a 20 amp breaker; #10 copper can be 30 amps, and so on.

The second thing to consider is that it's possible to create a fire hazard by *overloading an extension cord.* This occurs when too much current is fl owing in a conductor that's not heavy enough for the electrical load in amps. The circuit can be properly wired and its circuit breaker correctly rated, but if too much current flows through an extension cord whose wires are too small, the cord will heat up. Sometimes there is also a *voltage drop* over a longer extension cord, which could damage your tools.

Factsheet B2 – Extension Cord Facts

With the wide use of power tools on construction sites, flexible extension cords often are necessary. Because they are exposed, flexible, and unsecured, they are more susceptible to damage than is fixed wiring. Hazards are created when cords, cord connectors, receptacles, and cord- and plug connected equipment are improperly used and maintained. **Here are some factors on extension cord safety noted by OSHA.**

Strain Relief

- To reduce hazards, flexible cords must connect to devices and to fittings in ways that prevent tension at joints and terminal screws. Flexible cords are finely stranded for flexibility, so straining a cord can cause the strands of one conductor to loosen from under terminal screws and touch another conductor.

Cord Damage

- A flexible cord may be damaged by door or window edges, by staples and fastenings, by abrasion from adjacent materials, or simply by aging. If the electrical conductors become exposed, there is a danger of shocks, burns, or fire. Replace frayed or damaged cords. Avoid running cords over sharp corners and edges.

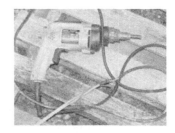

Durability

- The OSHA construction standard requires flexible cords to be rated for hard or extra-hard usage. These ratings are derived from the National Electrical Code, and are required to be indelibly marked approximately every foot along the length of the cord. Examples of these codes are: S, ST, SO, and STO for hard service, and SJ, SJO, SJT, and SJTO for junior hard service.

Grounding

- Extension cords must be 3-wire type so they may be grounded, and to permit grounding of any tools or equipment connected to them.

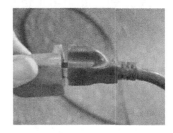

Wet Conditions

When a cord connector is wet, electric current can leak to the equipment grounding conductor, and to anyone who picks up that connectors if they provide a path to ground. Such leakage can occur not just on the face of the conductor, but at any wetter portion. Limit exposure of connectors and tools to excessive moisture by using watertight or sealable connectors.

ACCIDENT SUMMARY No. 11

Accident Type:	Electrocution
Weather Conditions:	Wet Ground
Type of Operation:	Remodeling
Size of Work Crew:	2
Collective Bargaining	No
Competent Safety Monitor on Site:	Yes
Safety and Health Program in Effect:	No
Was the Worksite Inspected Regularly:	Yes
Training and Education Provided:	No
Employee Job Title:	Carpenter
Age & Sex:	33-Male
Experience at this Type of Work:	30 Days
Time on Project:	3 Days

BRIEF DESCRIPTION OF ACCIDENT

Two employees were installing aluminum siding on a farmhouse when it became necessary to remove a 36-foot high metal pole CB antenna. One employee stood on a metal pick board between two ladders and unfastened the antenna at the top of the house. The other employee, who was standing on the ground, took the antenna to lay it down in the yard. The antenna made electrical contact with a 7200-volt power transmission tine 30 feet 10 inches from the house and 23 feet 9 inches above the ground. The employee handling the antenna received a fatal shock and the other employee a minor shock.

INSPECTION RESULTS

Following its investigation, OSHA issued one citation for two alleged serious violations of its construction standards. Had these standards been adhered to, the fatality might have been prevented.

ACCIDENT PREVENTION RECOMMENDATIONS

_____
_____
_____
_____
_____
_____
_____
_____
_____
_____
_____
_____

NOTE: The Fatal Facts were selected as being representative of fatalities caused by improper work practices. No special emphasis or priority is implied nor is the case necessarily a recent occurrence. The legal aspects of the incident have been resolved, and the case is now closed. Current as of: 11/01/2001.

ACCIDENT SUMMARY No. 17

Accident Type:	Electrocution
Weather Conditions:	Sunny, Clear
Type of Operation:	Steel Erection
Size of Work Crew:	3
Collective Bargaining	No
Competent Safety Monitor on Site:	Yes - Victim
Safety and Health Program in Effect:	No
Was the Worksite Inspected Regularly:	Yes
Training and Education Provided:	No
Employee Job Title:	Steel Erector Foreman
Age & Sex:	43-Male
Experience at this Type of Work:	4 months
Time on Project:	4 Hours

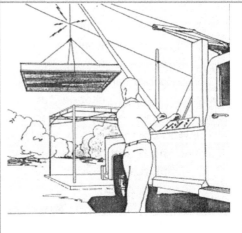

BRIEF DESCRIPTION OF ACCIDENT

Employees were moving a steel canopy structure using a "boom crane" truck. The boom cable made contact with a 7200 volt electrical power distribution line electrocuting the operator of the crane; he was the foreman at the site.

INSPECTION RESULTS

As a result of its investigation. OSHA issued citations for four serious violations of its construction standards dealing with training, protective equipment, and working too close to power lines. OSHA's construction safety standards include several requirements which, If they had been followed here. might have prevented this fatality.

ACCIDENT PREVENTION RECOMMENDATIONS

_____
_____
_____
_____
_____
_____
_____
_____
_____
_____
_____
_____

NOTE: *The Fatal Facts were selected as being representative of fatalities caused by improper work practices. No special emphasis or priority is implied nor is the case necessarily a recent occurrence. The legal aspects of the incident have been resolved, and the case is now closed. Current as of: 11/01/2001.*

ACCIDENT SUMMARY No. 28

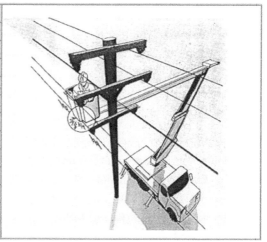

Accident Type:	Electrocution
Weather Conditions:	Clear
Type of Operation:	Power Line Work
Size of Work Crew:	2
Collective Bargaining	Yes
Competent Safety Monitor on Site:	Yes
Safety and Health Program in Effect:	No
Was the Worksite Inspected Regularly:	No
Training and Education Provided:	No
Employee Job Title:	Lineman
Age & Sex:	44-Male
Experience at this Type of Work:	11 Months
Time on Project:	6 Weeks

BRIEF DESCRIPTION OF ACCIDENT

A lineman was electrocuted while working on grounded de-energized lines. He was working from a defective basket on an articulated boom aerial lift when the basket contacted energized lines which ran beneath the de-energized lines. The defective basket permitted current to pass through a drain hole cut into the body of the basket, then through the employee, and to ground via the de-energized line.

INSPECTION RESULTS

OSHA cited the company for two serious violations and one other than serious violation of its construction standards. Had barriers been erected to prevent contact with adjacent energized lines, the electrical shock might have been prevented.

ACCIDENT PREVENTION RECOMMENDATIONS

_____
_____
_____
_____
_____
_____
_____
_____
_____
_____
_____
_____
_____
_____

NOTE: The Fatal Facts were selected as being representative of fatalities caused by improper work practices. No special emphasis or priority is implied nor is the case necessarily a recent occurrence. The legal aspects of the incident have been resolved, and the case is now closed. Current as of: 11/01/2001.

ACCIDENT SUMMARY No. 30

Accident Type:	Electrocution
Weather Conditions:	Raining
Type of Operation:	Electrical Contractor
Size of Work Crew:	2
Collective Bargaining	No
Competent Safety Monitor on Site:	Yes
Safety and Health Program in Effect:	Inadequate
Was the Worksite Inspected Regularly:	Yes
Training and Education Provided:	No
Employee Job Title:	Journeyman Electrician
Age & Sex:	39-Male
Experience at this Type of Work:	16 Years
Time on Project:	1 Day

BRIEF DESCRIPTION OF ACCIDENT

An electrician was removing metal fish tape from a hole at the base of a metal light pole. The fish tape became energized, electrocuting him.

INSPECTION RESULTS

As a result of its inspection, OSHA issued a citation for three serious violations of the agency's construction standards. Had requirements for de-energizing energy sources been followed, the electrocution might have been prevented.

ACCIDENT PREVENTION RECOMMENDATIONS

_____
_____
_____
_____
_____
_____
_____
_____
_____
_____
_____
_____
_____

ACCIDENT SUMMARY No. 40

Accident Type:	Electrocution	
Weather Conditions:	Sunny/Clear	
Type of Operation:	Fence Construction	
Size of Work Crew:	5	
Collective Bargaining	No	
Competent Safety Monitor on Site:	No	
Safety and Health Program in Effect:	Yes	
Was the Worksite Inspected Regularly:	No	
Training and Education Provided:	No	
Employee Job Title:	Laborer	
Age & Sex:	25-Male	
Experience at this Type of Work:	3 Months	
Time on Project:	1 Day	

BRIEF DESCRIPTION OF ACCIDENT

Five employees were constructing a chain link fence in front of a house and directly below a 7200-volt energized power line. They were installing 21-foot sections of metal top rail on the fence. One employee picked up a 21-foot section of top rail and held it up vertically. The top rail contacted the 7200-volt line, and the employee was electrocuted.

INSPECTION RESULTS

Following its inspection, OSHA determined that the employee who was killed had never received any safety training from his employer nor any specific instruction in avoiding the hazards posed by overhead power lines. The agency issued two serious citations for the training deficiencies.

ACCIDENT PREVENTION RECOMMENDATIONS

_____
_____
_____
_____
_____
_____
_____
_____
_____
_____
_____
_____

NOTE: _The Fatal Facts were selected as being representative of fatalities caused by improper work practices. No special emphasis or priority is implied nor is the case necessarily a recent occurrence. The legal aspects of the incident have been resolved, and the case is now closed. Current as of: 11/01/2001._

ACCIDENT SUMMARY No. 49

Accident Type:	Electrical Shock	
Weather Conditions:	Clear/Hot	
Type of Operation:	Masonry Contractor	
Size of Work Crew:	6	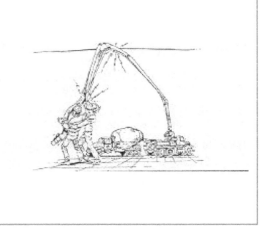
Collective Bargaining	No	
Competent Safety Monitor on Site:	No	
Safety and Health Program in Effect:	Inadequate	
Was the Worksite Inspected Regularly:	Yes	
Training and Education Provided:	No	
Employee Job Title:	Cement Finisher	
Age & Sex:	34-Male	
Experience at this Type of Work:	10 Years	
Time on Project:	1 Day	

BRIEF DESCRIPTION OF ACCIDENT

Two employees were spreading concrete as it was being delivered by 1 concrete pumper truck boom. The truck was parked across the street from the worksite. Overhead power lines ran perpendicular to the boom on the pumper truck. One employee was moving the hose (elephant trunk) to pour the concrete when the boom of the pumper truck came in contact with the overhead rover line carrying 7,620 volts. Employee received a fatal electric shock and fell on the other employee who was assisting him. The second employee received massive electrical shock and burns. * Safety training requirement was not being carried out at time of accident.

INSPECTION RESULTS

OSHA cited the employer for not instructing each employee to recognize and avoid unsafe conditions which apply to the work and work areas. Employer was also cited for operating equipment within ten feet of an energized electrical, ungrounded transmission lines rated 50 kV or less and not erecting insulating barriers.

ACCIDENT PREVENTION RECOMMENDATIONS

_____
_____
_____
_____
_____
_____
_____
_____
_____
_____
_____
_____

NOTE: *The Fatal Facts were selected as being representative of fatalities caused by improper work practices. No special emphasis or priority is implied nor is the case necessarily a recent occurrence. The legal aspects of the incident have been resolved, and the case is now closed. Current as of: 11/01/2001.*

ACCIDENT SUMMARY No. 57

Accident Type:	Electrocution
Weather Conditions:	Clear/Hot/Humid
Type of Operation:	Window Shutter Installers
Size of Work Crew:	2
Collective Bargaining	N/A
Competent Safety Monitor on Site:	No
Safety and Health Program in Effect:	Partial
Was the Worksite Inspected Regularly:	No
Training and Education Provided:	Some
Employee Job Title:	Helper
Age & Sex:	17-Male
Experience at this Type of Work:	One Month
Time on Project:	One Month

BRIEF DESCRIPTION OF ACCIDENT

One employee was climbing a metal ladder to hand an electric drill to the journeyman installer on a scaffold about five feet above him. When the victim reached the third rung from the bottom of the ladder he received an electric shock that killed him. The investigation revealed that the extension cord had a missing grounding prong and that a conductor on the green grounding wire was making intermittent contact with the energizing black wire thereby energizing the entire length of the grounding wire and the drill's frame. The drill was not double insulated.

INSPECTION RESULTS

As a result of its investigation, OSHA issued citations for violations of construction standards.

ACCIDENT PREVENTION RECOMMENDATIONS

_____
_____
_____
_____
_____
_____
_____
_____
_____
_____
_____
_____

NOTE: _The Fatal Facts were selected as being representative of fatalities caused by improper work practices. No special emphasis or priority is implied nor is the case necessarily a recent occurrence. The legal aspects of the incident have been resolved, and the case is now closed. Current as of: 11/01/2001._

ACCIDENT SUMMARY No. 60

Accident Type:	Electrocution
Weather Conditions:	Indoor Work
Type of Operation:	Installing and Trouble-shooting overhead lamps
Size of Work Crew:	15
Competent Safety Monitor on Site:	Yes
Safety and Health Program in Effect:	Inadequate
Was the Worksite Inspected Regularly:	Yes
Training and Education Provided:	No
Employee Job Title:	Electrician
Age & Sex:	53-Male
Experience at this Type of Work:	Journeyman
Time on Project:	1 Month

BRIEF DESCRIPTION OF ACCIDENT

The employee was attempting to correct an electrical problem involving two non-operational lamps. He proceeded to the area where he thought the problem was. He had not shut off the power at the circuit breaker panel nor had he tested the wires to see if they were live. He was electrocuted when he grabbed the two live wires with his left hand and then fell from the ladder.

INSPECTION RESULTS

As a result of its investigation, OSHA Issued citations alleging three serious violations. OSHA's construction standards include several requirements which, if they had been followed here, might have prevented this fatality.

ACCIDENT PREVENTION RECOMMENDATIONS

_____
_____
_____
_____
_____
_____
_____
_____
_____
_____
_____
_____

NOTE: _The case here described was selected as being representative of fatalities caused by improper work practices. No special emphasis or priority is implied nor is the case necessarily a recent occurrence. The legal aspects of the incident have been resolved, and the case is now closed._

Recognize Any Hazard(s)?

_____

_____

_____

_____

_____

_____

_____

Recognize Any Hazard(s)?

_____

_____

_____

_____

_____

_____

_____

_____

Recognize Any Hazard(s)?

_____

_____

_____

_____

_____

_____

_____

_____

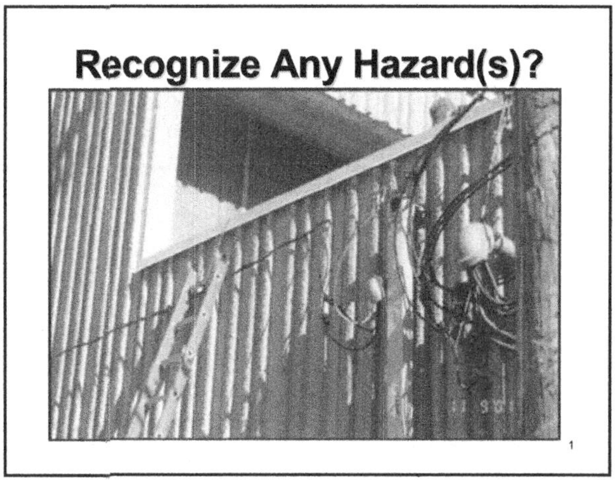

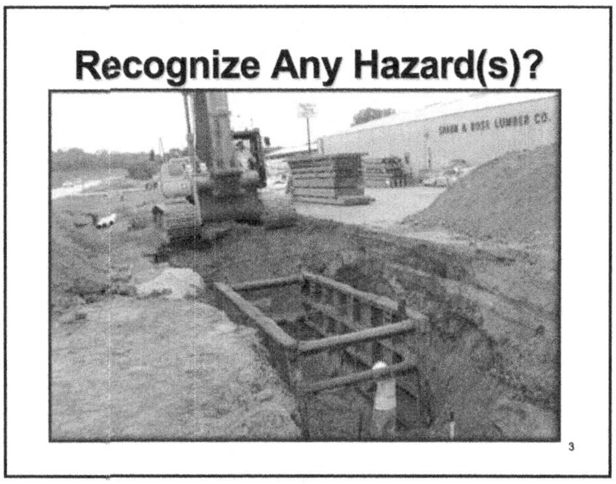

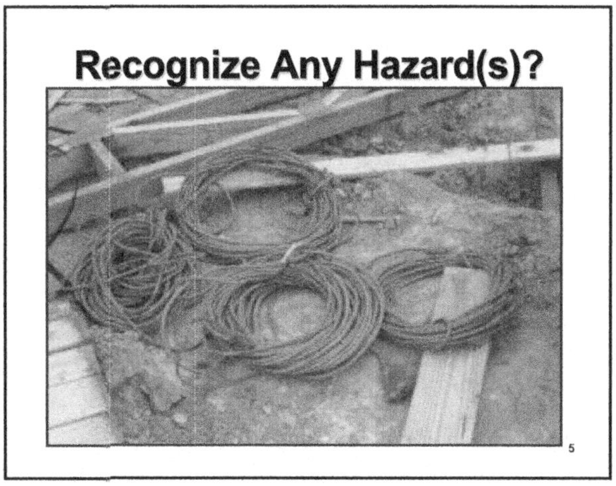

Recognize Any Hazard(s)?

Recognize Any Hazard(s)?

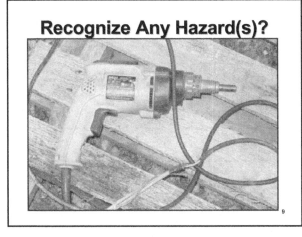

Recognize Any Hazard(s)?

Recognize Any Hazard(s)?

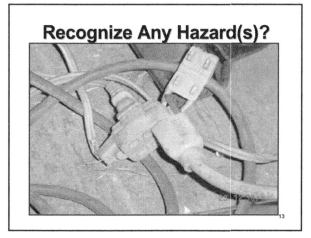

_____

_____

_____

_____

_____

_____

_____

Recognize Any Hazard(s)?

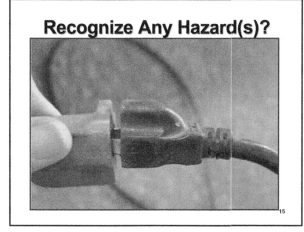

_____

_____

_____

_____

_____

_____

_____

Recognize Any Hazard(s)?

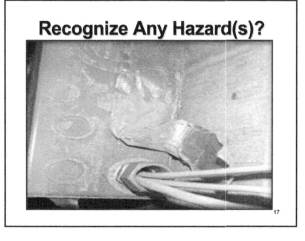

_____

_____

_____

_____

_____

_____

_____

Recognize Any Hazard(s)?

Construction Focus Four: Electrocution Hazards Lesson Test

NAME: _____   DATE: ___/___/___

1. "BE SAFE" reminds workers that burns, electrocution, shock, arc flash/arc blast, fire and explosions are all:
   a. Electrical hazards workers are exposed to when working around cranes and power lines.
   b. Serious workplace hazards that workers are exposed to when working in and/or around electrical power sources.
   c. Electrical hazards workers are exposed to when working with flammables.

2. A ground fault circuit interrupter (GFCI):
   a. Detects ground faults and interrupts the flow of electric current, and is designed to protect the worker by limiting the duration of an electrical shock.
   b. Detects ground faults and interrupts the electric source thus, it disables the equipment that is attached; however, the worker is still exposed to electrocution.
   c. A tool used to determine if a power system is properly grounded.

3. To protect yourself from being electrocuted by contact with overhead power lines, you should always assume overhead lines are energized and keep yourself and equipment at least _____ away from power lines up to 50kV.
   a. 5 feet
   b. 8 feet
   c. 10 feet

4. Which of the following is a safe work practice to protect you from electrocution hazards?
   a. Use GFCI only when using double insulated power tools
   b. Do not operate electrical equipment when working in wet conditions
   c. Attach ungrounded, two-prong adapter plugs to three-prong cords and tools

5. Some requirements employers must do to protect workers from electrocution hazards are: ensure overhead power lines safety; supply GFCIs; isolate electrical parts; ensure proper grounding, and:
   1. Provide training
   2. Ensure power tools are maintained in a safe condition
   3. Ensure proper use of flexible cords
   4. Report worker jobsite complaints to OSHA

   a. 1, 2, and 3
   b. 2, 3, and 4
   c. 1, 3 and 4

6. When a power system is properly grounded workers need to be aware that:
   a. It is a safe system and can not change from safe to hazardous; therefore working with electrical equipment is always safe.
   b. Electrical equipment can instantly change from safe to hazardous because of extreme conditions and rough treatment.
   c. The system will remain safe and will not be impacted by changing worksite conditions or electrical equipment.

Focus 4: Struck-by

How to prevent injury

◆ Ask for a nail gun with a sequential trigger mechanism.

◆ NEVER shoot towards yourself or a co-worker.

◆ Do not press the trigger unless the nose of the gun (contact element) is firmly pressed against the work material.

◆ NEVER walk around with your finger on the trigger.

◆ NEVER clean or clear jams or adjust a nail gun when it is connected to the air supply.

◆ Avoid nailing into knots and metal; nails are more likely to ricochet. Dense materials, like laminated beams, are also difficult to nail.

◆ NEVER remove or bypass safety devices, triggers, or contact springs.

◆ NEVER use a defective tool. If a tool is malfunctioning, it needs to be tagged and taken out of service.

To read stories about nail gun injuries and see photos, visit
www.cpwr.com/nailguns

To learn more about CPWR, visit
www.cpwr.com

For more safety and health information, visit
www.elcosh.org

CPWR
8484 Georgia Ave, Suite 1000
Silver Spring, MD 20910
301-578-8500

© 2008, CPWR – The Center for Construction Research and Training. All rights reserved. CPWR is the research, training, and service arm of the Building and Construction Trades Dept., AFL-CIO, and works to reduce or eliminate safety and health hazards construction workers face on the job. Production of this card was supported by Grant OH008307 from the National Institute for Occupational Safety and Health (NIOSH). The contents are solely the responsibility of the authors and do not necessarily represent the official views of NIOSH.

HAZARD ALERT

Nail Guns

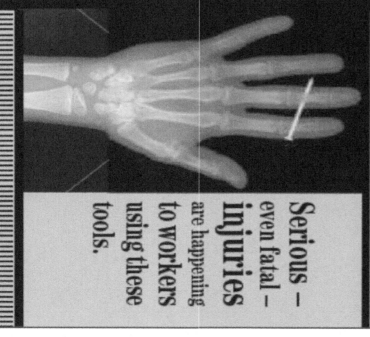

Serious – even fatal – injuries are happening to workers using these tools.

68

What's the problem?

Nail guns are popular for a reason. They get the job done in a blink of an eye.

But that rapid-fire action can work against you. In a split second, a nail can enter your finger, your hand, or worse.

Nail gun injuries are much more common than people think. Most injuries involve puncture wounds to hands or fingers, but serious, even fatal, injuries are also associated with the use of these tools.

How most nail gun injuries happen

◆ Accidental or unintended firing, often associated with recoil of the tool after firing

◆ Ricocheting nails

◆ Nail going through work surface

◆ Airborne nails

◆ By-passed safety features

◆ Unsafe work practices

◆ Holding finger on contact trigger

Basic information about nail guns

Although there are many types of nail guns (framing, finishing, flooring, etc.), there are two common triggers:

Contact trip trigger mechanisms allow the tool to fire anytime the trigger and the nose of the gun (contact element) are both depressed. Trigger can be held down to allow bump or bounce nailing.

Sequential triggers require the nose of gun (contact element) to be depressed before the trigger is pulled. That avoids inadvertent discharge of nails.

WARNING:

The two triggers look exactly alike. You will not be able to tell the difference!

If you can "bump nail" by holding the trigger down, and bouncing the nose against a nailing surface, that is a contact trigger gun.
Use extreme caution.

Why it's important:

1) The contact trip trigger mechanism carries twice the risk of the sequential trigger, even after considering experience and training.

2) Accidental firings are most common following recoil of tools with contact trip triggers.

3) If you are not trained in using either of these tools, you are at high risk of injury.

"Faster" trigger does not increase productivity

A recent study measuring productivity in construction found that the contact trip trigger showed no significant difference (less than 1 percent) in productivity than the sequential trigger. Also, there was no significant difference between the two tools in nail count and placement.

The study, which involved journeymen carpenters with an average of 13 years in the trade, found that the difference in productivity was the worker, not the tool.

Cranes and rigging

Properly securing any load with appropriate rigging is crucial to any lifting being done by machinery on the job-site. If the rigging fails the results can cause serious injury and even death. Before any load is lifted all components of the rigging hardware should be evaluated to ensure they can withstand the forces of the load.

Follow these safe work practices

1. Guard all exposed gears, rotating shafts, pulleys, sprockets or other moving parts to prevent contact with employees.

2. Guard or block the swing radius of the crane to restrict and prevent employees from entering into and being struck by the machine.

3. Inspect all rigging equipment prior to each lift, this should include all slings, chains, ropes, and like materials used to support and lift materials.

4. Remove from service any defective equipment immediately.

5. Be sure to inspect all hooks, clamps, and other lifting accessories for their rated load.

6. Clearly communicate to all employees on site that no one is permitted to work under loads.

7. Be sure the person responsible for signaling the crane operator stays in visual contact with the operator and has been trained to use the correct signals.

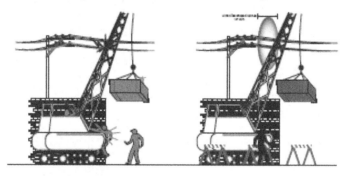

WRONG WAY   RIGHT WAY

www.buildsafe.org
16 — English

PPE for Workers Checklist

Protection	TYPICAL OPERATIONS OF CONCERN	YES	NO
EYE	Sawing, cutting, drilling, sanding, grinding, hammering, chopping, abrasive blasting, punch press operations, etc.		
	Pouring, mixing, painting, cleaning, siphoning, dip tank operations, dental and health care services, etc.		
	Battery charging, installing fiberglass insulation, compressed air or gas operations, etc.		
	Welding, cutting, laser operations, etc.		
FACE	Pouring, mixing, painting, cleaning, siphoning, dip tank operations, etc.		
	Welding, pouring molten metal, smithing, baking, cooking, drying, etc.		
	Cutting, sanding, grinding, hammering, chopping, pouring, mixing, painting, cleaning, siphoning, etc.		
HEAD	Work stations or traffic routes located under catwalks or conveyor belts, construction, trenching, utility work, etc.		
	Construction, confined space operations, building maintenance, etc.		
	Building maintenance; utility work; construction; wiring; work on or near communications, computer, or other high tech equipment; arc or resistance welding; etc.		
FEET	Construction, plumbing, smithing, building maintenance, trenching, utility work, grass cutting, etc.		
	Building maintenance; utility work; construction; wiring; work on or near communications, computer, or other high tech equipment; arc or resistance welding; etc.		
	Welding, foundry work, casting, smithing, etc.		
	Demolition, explosives manufacturing, grain milling, spray painting, abrasive blasting, work with highly flammable materials, etc.		
HANDS	Grinding, sanding, sawing, hammering, material handling, etc.		
	Pouring, mixing, painting, cleaning, siphoning, dip tank operations, health care and dental services, etc.		
	Welding, pouring molten metal, smithing, baking, cooking, drying, etc.		
	Building maintenance; utility work; construction; wiring; work on or near communications, computer, or other high tech equipment; arc or resistance welding; etc.		
BODY	Pouring, mixing, painting, cleaning, siphoning, dip tank operations, machining, sawing, battery charging, installing fiberglass insulation, compressed air or gas operations, etc.		
	Cutting, grinding, sanding, sawing, glazing, material handling, etc.		
	Welding, pouring molten metal, smithing, baking, cooking, drying, etc.		
	Pouring, mixing, painting, cleaning, siphoning, dip tank operations, etc.		
HEARING	Machining, grinding, sanding, work near conveyors, pneumatic equipment, generators, ventilation fans, motors, punch and brake presses, etc. Samples shown are: ear muffs (left) and earplugs (right)		

NOTE: Pictures of PPE are intended to provide a small sample of what the protection gear may look like. They are not to scale nor are they inclusive of all protection gear required and/or that is available.

OPTION A: Focus Four Toolbox Talks 1 [Student copy]

Actual Incident:
A 36-year-old construction inspector for the county died when an asphalt dump truck backed over him. The inspector was wearing an orange reflective vest and hard-hat and the dump truck had a backup alarm that was functioning. The truck traveled approximately 770 feet in reverse.

How do we prevent these results?

_____
_____
_____
_____
_____
_____
_____
_____
_____
_____
_____
_____
_____
_____
_____
_____
_____
_____
_____
_____
_____
_____
_____

Additional discussion notes:

_____
_____
_____
_____

Actual Incident:
A 56-year-old truck driver was crushed when a crane tipped over and the crane's boom landed on the cab of the dump truck in which he was sitting. The crane had been lowering an empty 4-yard concrete bucket, while booming out.

How do we prevent these results?

_____
_____
_____
_____
_____
_____
_____
_____
_____
_____
_____
_____
_____
_____
_____
_____
_____
_____
_____
_____
_____
_____
_____
_____
_____

Additional discussion notes:

_____
_____
_____
_____

ACCIDENT SUMMARY No. 2

Accident Type:	Struck by Nail
Weather Conditions:	N/A
Type of Company:	General Contractors
Size of Work Crew:	17
Union or Non-union:	Union
Worksite Inspection?:	No
Designated Competent Person on Site?:	No
Employer Safety and Health Program?:	No
Training and Education for Employees?:	No
Craft of Deceased Employee(s):	Carpenter
Age; Sex	22; Male
Time of the Job:	3:00 p.m.
Time at the Task	Unknown

BRIEF DESCRIPTION OF ACCIDENT

A carpenter apprentice was killed when he was struck in the head by a nail that was fired from a powder actuated tool. The tool operator, while attempting to anchor a plywood form in preparation for pouring a concrete wall, fired the gun causing the nail to pass through the hollow wall. The nail travelled some twenty-seven feet before striking the victim. The tool operator had never received training in the proper use of the tool, and none of the employees in the area were wearing personal protective equipment.

INSPECTION RESULTS

Section not listed on original

ACCIDENT PREVENTION RECOMMENDATIONS

_____
_____
_____
_____
_____
_____
_____
_____
_____
_____
_____
_____
_____

NOTE: The case here described was selected as being representative of fatalities caused by improper work practices. No special emphasis or priority is implied nor is the case necessarily a recent occurrence. The legal aspects of the incident have been resolved, and the case is now closed.

ACCIDENT SUMMARY No. 4

Accident Type:	Struck by Collapsing Crane Boom
Weather Conditions:	Clear
Type of Company:	General Contractor
Size of Work Crew:	9
Union or Non-union:	Union
Worksite Inspections Conducted:	Yes
Designated Competent Person on Site (1926.20(b)(2)):	Yes
Employer Safety Health Program:	Yes
Training and Education for Employees:	Yes
Craft of Deceased Employee(s):	3. Iron Worker 4. Management Trainee
Age & Sex	3. Ironworker-35; male 4. Management Trainee-26; male
Time on the Job:	1 hour
Time on Task:	1 hour

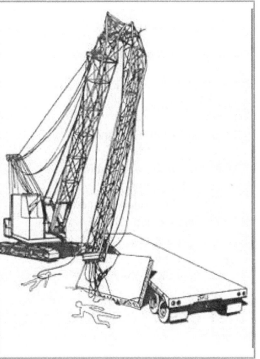

BRIEF DESCRIPTION OF ACCIDENT

A crew of ironworkers and a crane operator were unloading a 20-ton steel slab from a low-boy trailer using a 50-ton crawler crane with 90-foot lattice boom. The operator was inexperienced on this crane and did not know the length of the boom. Further, no one had determined the load radius. During lifting, the load moved forward and to the right, placing a twisting force on the boom. The boom twisted under the load, swinging down, under and to the right. Two employees standing 30 feet away apparently saw the boom begin to swing and ran. The boom struck one of the employees - an ironworker - on the head, causing instant death. Wire rope struck the other -- a management trainee -- causing internal injuries. He died two hours later at a local hospital.

INSPECTION RESULTS

Section not listed on original

ACCIDENT PREVENTION RECOMMENDATIONS

_____

_____

_____

_____

NOTE: *The case here described was selected as being representative of fatalities caused by improper work practices. No special emphasis or priority is implied nor is the case necessarily a recent occurrence. The legal aspects of the incident have been resolved, and the case is now closed.*

ACCIDENT SUMMARY No. 8

Accident Type:	Struck by Falling Object
Weather Conditions:	Clear
Type of Operation:	Transmission Tower Construction
Size of Work Crew:	4
Union or Non-union	Union
Competent Safety Monitor on Site:	Yes
Safety and Health Program in Effect:	Yes
Was the Worksite Inspected Regularly:	Yes
Training and Education Provided:	No
Employee Job Title:	Groundman (Framer)
Age & Sex:	24-Male
Experience at this Type of Work:	2 Years
Time on Project:	3 Days

BRIEF DESCRIPTION OF ACCIDENT

Ball and socket connectors are used to attach conductor stringing blocks to insulators on the arms of 90 foot metal towers of electrical transmission lines. Normally stainless steel cotter keys secure the ball and socket connector in place. In this case, however, black electrical tape was wrapped around the socket to keep the ball in place rather than a cotter key. The tape apparently stretched and the ball came loose, dropping the stringing block approximately 90 feet onto the head of an employee below, one of a four-man erection crew.

INSPECTION RESULTS

As result of the its investigation, OSHA issued citations alleging three serious and two other-than-serious violations.

OSHA's construction safety standards include several requirements which, if they had been followed here, might have prevented this fatality.

ACCIDENT PREVENTION RECOMMENDATIONS

_____

_____

_____

_____

_____

_____

NOTE: _The case here described was selected as being representative of fatalities caused by improper work practices. No special emphasis or priority is implied nor is the case necessarily a recent occurrence. The legal aspects of the incident have been resolved, and the case is now closed._

76

ACCIDENT SUMMARY No. 51

Accident Type:	Struck By
Weather Conditions:	Clear/Cool/Windy
Type of Operation:	Construction Maintainence
Size of Work Crew:	3
Collective Bargaining	Yes
Competent Safety Monitor on Site:	No
Safety and Health Program in Effect:	No
Was the Worksite Inspected Regularly:	Inadequate*
Training and Education Provided:	No
Employee Job Title:	Laborer
Age & Sex:	33-Male
Experience at this Type of Work:	18 Weeks
Time on Project:	1 Day

BRIEF DESCRIPTION OF ACCIDENT

Employees were dismantling grain spouts at a grain elevator. Sections of the spout were connected by collars. A ten foot section of a spout weighing 600 pounds was being pulled through a vent hole by a 5-ton winch. As the spout was being pulled through the opening to the outside, the spout became wedged at the point where the collar was to pass through. Several employees used pry bars to free the collar which was under tension. The spout popped out of the vent striking and killing an employee who was standing beside the spout. * Employer provided but did not require use of hard hats.

INSPECTION RESULTS

As a result of its investigation, OSHA issued two citations alleging serious violations. The employee should have been able to recognize that this situation was hazardous. Additionally, the investigation revealed that this employee was not wearing personal protective equipment in this hazardous situation. Had he been wearing a hard hat this death might have been prevented.

ACCIDENT PREVENTION RECOMMENDATIONS

_____
_____
_____
_____
_____
_____

NOTE: *The case here described was selected as being representative of fatalities caused by improper work practices. No special emphasis or priority is implied nor is the case necessarily a recent occurrence. The legal aspects of the incident have been resolved, and the case is now closed.*

Recognize Any Hazard(s)?

Source: OTI Course #3030

_____

_____

_____

_____

_____

_____

Recognize Any Hazard(s)?

Source: Susan Harwood Grant Number SH-17792-08-60-F-48 by Compacion Foundation

_____

_____

_____

_____

_____

_____

_____

Recognize Any Hazard(s)?

Source: Construction Safety Council

_____

_____

_____

_____

_____

_____

_____

Recognize Any Hazard(s)?

Source: National Photo Archive ID #3295

7

Recognize Any Hazard(s)?

Source: National Photo Archive ID #1470

9

Recognize Any Hazard(s)?

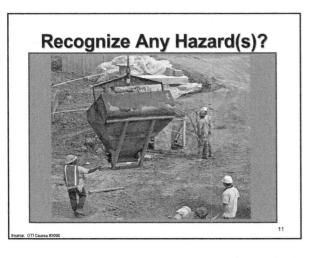

Source: OTI Course #2000

11

Recognize Any Hazard(s)?

Source: National Photo Archive ID #3486

13

Recognize Any Hazard(s)?

Source: National Photo Archive ID #1860

15

Recognize Any Hazard(s)?

Source: OTI Course #2080

17

Recognize Any Hazard(s)?

Construction Focus Four: Struck-By Hazards Lesson Test

NAME: _____   DATE: ___/___/___

1. Struck-by injuries are produced by forcible contact or impact between the injured person and a/n _____.
   a. High voltage power line or other energy source
   b. Object or piece of equipment
   c. Co-worker or employer

2. The following are examples of struck-by hazards. Which one is an example of a struck-by <u>flying</u> hazard?
   a. Hit by a nail from a nail gun
   b. Hit by a load dropped from a crane
   c. Run over by a vehicle in a roadway work zone

3. As a load is mechanically lifted, the materials _____.
   a. May strike workers if the load swings, twists or turns
   b. Will not be affected by windy conditions or bad weather
   c. Can weigh any amount without causing a problem with the equipment

4. Among the list of ways workers can protect themselves when working on or near any construction zone, is to _____.
   a. Direct traffic in and out of the work zone
   b. Work behind moving vehicles
   c. Wear high-visibility reflective clothing

5. A struck-by hazard can be described as anytime a worker _____.
   a. Falls from a height of greater than ten feet
   b. Is hit by a falling, swinging, flying or rolling object
   c. Can get any part of his/her body caught in or in between objects

6. Employers must protect workers from struck-by hazards by _____.
   a. Providing PPE such as hard hats and safety glasses
   b. Establishing guidelines that allow only contractors access in the crane work zone
   c. Ensuring guards on tools and equipment are removed when it is absolutely necessary to get the job done

Focus 4: Caught-in or -between

ACCIDENT SUMMARY No. 5

Accident Type:	Caught in or Between	
Weather Conditions:	Clear	
Type of Company:	Street Paving Contractor	
Size of Work Crew:	1	
Union or Non-union:	Non-Union	
Worksite Inspections Conducted (1926.20(b)(2)):	Yes	
Designated Competent Person on Site (1926.20(b)(2)):	Yes	
Employer Safety Health Program:	Yes	
Training and Education for Employees (1926.21(b)):	Yes	
Craft of Deceased Employee(s):	Ironworker	
Age & Sex:	22-Male	
Time on the Job:	1 day	
Time on Task:	3 Hours	

BRIEF DESCRIPTION OF ACCIDENT

A laborer was steam cleaning a scraper. The bowl apron had been left in the raised position. The hydraulically controlled apron had not been blocked to prevent it from accidently falling. The apron did fall unexpectedly and the employee was caught between the apron and the cutting edge of the scraper bowl. The apron weighted approximately 2500 pounds.

ACCIDENT PREVENTION RECOMMENDATIONS

FATAL FACTS

ACCIDENT SUMMARY No. 13

Accident Type:	Collapse of Shoring	
Weather Conditions:	Clear	
Type of Operation:	Boring and Pipe Jacking Excavation	
Size of Work Crew:	4	
Collective Bargaining	Yes	
Competent Safety Monitor on Site:	Yes	
Safety and Health Program in Effect:	No	
Was the Worksite Inspected Regularly:	Yes	
Training and Education Provided:	Yes	
Employee Job Title:	Pipe Welder	
Age & Sex:	62-Male	
Experience at this Type of Work:	18 years	
Time on Project:	2½	

BRIEF DESCRIPTION OF ACCIDENT

Four employees were boring a hole and pushing a 20-inch pipe casing under a road. The employees were in an excavation approximately 9 feet wide, 32 feet long and 7 feet deep. Steel plates 8' × 15' × ¾", being used as shoring, were placed vertically against the north and south walls of the excavation at approximately a 30 degree angle. There were no horizontal braces between the steel plates. The steel plate on the south wall tipped over, pinning an employee (who was killed) between the steel plate and the pipe casing. At the time the plate tipped over, a backhoe was being operated adjacent to the excavation.

ACCIDENT PREVENTION RECOMMENDATIONS

ACCIDENT SUMMARY No. 15

Accident Type:	Crushed by Dump Truck Body	
Weather Conditions:	Clear, Warm	
Type of Operation:	General Contractor	
Size of Work Crew:	N/A	
Collective Bargaining	Yes	
Competent Safety Monitor on Site:	Yes	
Safety and Health Program in Effect:	Yes	
Was the Worksite Inspected Regularly:	Yes	
Training and Education Provided:	No	
Employee Job Title:	Truck Driver	
Age & Sex:	25-Male	
Experience at this Type of Work:	2 Months	
Time on Project:	2 Weeks at Site	

BRIEF DESCRIPTION OF ACCIDENT

A truck driver was crushed and killed between the frame and dump box of a dump truck. Apparently a safety "over-travel" cable attached between the truck frame and the dump box malfunctioned by catching on a protruding nut of an air brake cylinder. This prevented the dump box from being fully raised, halting its progress at a point where about 20 inches of space remained between it and the truck frame. The employee, apparently assuming that releasing the cable would allow the dump box to continue up-ward, reached between the rear dual wheels and over the frame, and disengaged the cable with his right hand. The dump box then dropped suddenly, crushing his head. The employee had not received training or instruction in proper operating procedures and was not made aware of all potential hazards in his work.

ACCIDENT PREVENTION RECOMMENDATIONS

ACCIDENT REPORT

ACCIDENT SUMMARY No. 18

Accident Type:	Caught by Rotating Part
Weather Conditions:	Clear
Type of Operation:	Telephone Line Installation
Size of Work Crew:	3
Collective Bargaining	No
Competent Safety Monitor on Site:	Yes - Victim
Safety and Health Program in Effect:	Yes
Was the Worksite Inspected Regularly:	Yes
Training and Education Provided:	No
Employee Job Title:	Boring Machine Operator
Age & Sex:	56-Male
Experience at this Type of Work:	10 Years
Time on Project:	5 Days

BRIEF DESCRIPTION OF ACCIDENT

A three-man crew was installing an underground telephone cable in a residential area. They had just completed a bore hole under a driveway using a horizontal boring machine. The bore hole rod had been removed from the hole. While the rod was still rotating, the operator straddled it and stooped over to pick it up. His trouser leg became entangled in the rotating rod and he was flipped over. He struck tools and materials, sustaining fatal injuries.

ACCIDENT PREVENTION RECOMMENDATIONS

ACCIDENT SUMMARY No. 22

Accident Type:	Cave-in	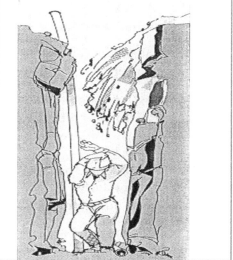
Weather Conditions:	Warm, Clear	
Type of Operation:	Excavator	
Size of Work Crew:	2	
Collective Bargaining	No	
Competent Safety Monitor on Site:	Yes	
Safety and Health Program in Effect:	No	
Was the Worksite Inspected Regularly:	Yes	
Training and Education Provided:	No	
Employee Job Title:	Laborer	
Age & Sex:	37-Male	
Experience at this Type of Work:	3 Years	
Time on Project:	2 Days	

BRIEF DESCRIPTION OF ACCIDENT

An employee was installing a small diameter pipe in a trench 3 feet wide, 12-15 feet deep and 90 feet long. The trench was not shored or sloped nor was there a box or shield to protect the employee. Further, there was evidence of a previous cave-in. The employee apparently reentered the trench, and a second cave-in occurred, burying him. He was found face down m the bottom of the trench.

ACCIDENT PREVENTION RECOMMENDATIONS

_____
_____
_____
_____
_____
_____
_____
_____
_____
_____
_____
_____
_____
_____
_____
_____
_____
_____

ACCIDENT SUMMARY No. 31

Accident Type:	Cave-in	
Weather Conditions:	Cloudy and Dry	
Type of Operation:	Trenching and excavation	
Size of Work Crew:	4	
Collective Bargaining	No	
Competent Safety Monitor on Site:	Yes	
Safety and Health Program in Effect:	Yes	
Was the Worksite Inspected Regularly:	Yes	
Training and Education Provided:	No	
Employee Job Title:	Pipe Layer	
Age & Sex:	32-Male	
Experience at this Type of Work:	9 Months	
Time on Project:	2 Weeks	

BRIEF DESCRIPTION OF ACCIDENT

Employees were laying sewer pipe in a trench 15 feet deep. The sides of the trench, 4 feet wide at the bottom and 15 feet wide at the top, were not shored or protected to prevent a cave-in. Soil in the lower portion of the trench was mostly sand and gravel and the upper portion was clay and loam*. The trench was not protected from vibration caused by heavy vehicle traffic on the road nearby. To leave the trench, employees had to exit by climbing over the backfill. As they attempted to leave the trench, there was a small cave-in covering one employee to his ankles. When the other employee went to his co-worker's aid another cave-in occurred covering him to his waist. The first employee died of a rupture of the right ventricle of his heart at the scene of the cave-in. The other employee suffered a hip injury.

ACCIDENT PREVENTION RECOMMENDATIONS

----

* Clay and loam are terms not used any longer; Soil condition is now described using A, B, or C

89

ACCIDENT SUMMARY No. 38

Accident Type:	Caught in or between
Weather Conditions:	Clear, dry
Type of Operation:	Highway, street construction
Size of Work Crew:	4
Collective Bargaining	Yes
Competent Safety Monitor on Site:	Yes
Safety and Health Program in Effect:	Yes
Was the Worksite Inspected Regularly:	Yes
Training and Education Provided:	No
Employee Job Title:	Equipment Operator
Age & Sex:	38-Male
Experience at this Type of Work:	11 Months
Time on Project:	1 Hour

BRIEF DESCRIPTION OF ACCIDENT

An employee was driving a front-end loader up a dirt ramp onto a lowboy trailer. The tractor tread began to slide off the trailer. As the tractor began to tip, the operator, who was not wearing a seat belt, jumped from the cab. As he hit the ground, the tractor's rollover protective structure fell on top of him, crushing him.

ACCIDENT PREVENTION RECOMMENDATIONS

ACCIDENT REPORT

FATAL FACTS

ACCIDENT SUMMARY No. 50

Accident Type:	Caught between Backhoe Superstructure and Concrete Wall
Weather Conditions:	Clear/Cool
Type of Operation:	Excavation Contractor
Size of Work Crew:	9
Collective Bargaining	Yes
Competent Safety Monitor on Site:	No
Safety and Health Program in Effect:	No
Was the Worksite Inspected Regularly:	No
Training and Education Provided:	No
Employee Job Title:	Truck Driver
Age & Sex:	34-Male
Experience at this Type of Work:	Unknown
Time on Project:	4 Days

Picture used may not be representative of a backhoe as indicated in the report

BRIEF DESCRIPTION OF ACCIDENT

The contractor was operating a backhoe when an employee attempted to walk between the swinging superstructure of the backhoe and a concrete wall. As the employee approached the backhoe from the operator's blind side, the superstructure hit the victim crushing him against the wall.

ACCIDENT PREVENTION RECOMMENDATIONS

_____
_____
_____
_____
_____
_____
_____
_____
_____
_____
_____
_____
_____
_____
_____
_____

ACCIDENT SUMMARY No. 61

Accident Type:	Trench Collapse	
Weather Conditions:	Fair	
Type of Operation:	Excavation Work	
Size of Work Crew:	2	
Competent Safety Monitor on Site:	No	
Safety and Health Program in Effect:	No	
Was the Worksite Inspected Regularly:	No	
Training and Education Provided:	Inadequate	
Employee Job Title:	Laborer	
Age & Sex:	51-Male	
Experience at this Type of Work:	6 Months	
Time on Project:	2 Days	

BRIEF DESCRIPTION OF ACCIDENT

An employee was working in a trench 4 feet wide and 7 feet deep. About 30 feet away a backhoe was straddling the trench when the backhoe operator noticed a large chunk of dirt falling from the side wall behind the worker in the trench, he called out a warning. Before the worker could climb out, 6 to 8 feet of the trench wall had collapsed on him and covered his body up to his neck. He suffocated before the backhoe operator could dig him out. There were no exit ladders. No sloping, shoring or other protective system had been used in the trench.

ACCIDENT PREVENTION RECOMMENDATIONS

_____
_____
_____
_____
_____
_____
_____
_____
_____
_____
_____
_____
_____
_____

ACCIDENT SUMMARY No. 73

Accident Type:	Struck by/Caught between	
Weather Conditions:	Clear/warm	
Type of Operation:	Stacking Structural Steel	
Size of Work Crew:	6	
Competent Person on Site:	No	
Safety and Health Program in Effect:	No	
Was the Worksite Inspected Regularly by the Employer:	No	
Training and Education Provided:	No	
Employee Job Title:	Laborer	
Age & Sex:	28-Male	
Experience at this Type of Work:	4 Years	
Time on Project:	5 Weeks	

BRIEF DESCRIPTION OF ACCIDENT

Two laborers and a fork lift driver were staking 40-foot-long I-beams in preparation for structural steel erection. One laborer was placing a 2 X 4 inch wooden spacer on the last I-beam on the stack. The fork lift driver drove up to the stack with another I-beam that was not secured or blocked on the fork lift tines. The I-beam fell from the tines, pining the laborer between the fallen I beam and the stack of beams.

ACCIDENT PREVENTION RECOMMENDATIONS

_____
_____
_____
_____
_____
_____
_____
_____
_____
_____
_____
_____
_____
_____
_____
_____

Caught-In or –Between Hazard Recognition
Student Copy
Take notes and record the details of the hazards that may be present

Recognize Any Hazard(s)?

Source: Southwest Safety Training Alliance

1

_____

_____

_____

_____

_____

_____

_____

Recognize Any Hazard(s)?

Source: Compacion Foundation (HCAdetejas.org)

3

_____

_____

_____

_____

_____

_____

_____

Recognize Any Hazard(s)?

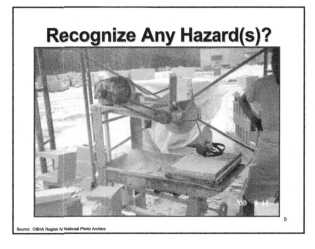

Source: OSHA Region IV National Photo Archive

5

_____

_____

_____

_____

_____

_____

_____

Recognize Any Hazard(s)?

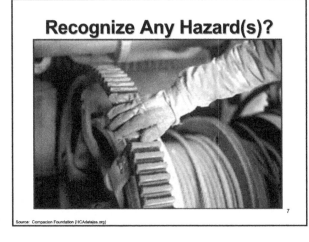

Source: Compacion Foundation (HCAdetajas.org)

7

_____
_____
_____
_____
_____
_____
_____

Recognize Any Hazard(s)?

Source: OSHA Directorate of Construction

9

_____
_____
_____
_____
_____
_____
_____

Recognize Any Hazard(s)?

Source: Indian River Community (now State) College

11

_____
_____
_____
_____
_____
_____
_____

Recognize Any Hazard(s)?

Source: Indian River Community (now State) College

Recognize Any Hazard(s)?

Source: Indian River Community (now State) College

Recognize Any Hazard(s)?

Source: Construction Safety Council

Recognize Any Hazard(s)?

Source: OSHA Region IV National Photo Archive

19

97

NAME: _____   DATE: ___/___/___

REVIEW EXERCISE – STUDENT COPY

Complete the following sentences using words from the word bank.

WORD BANK		
Safety guard	Identifying	5 feet
Cave-in	Stacked	Corrective	Secured
Equipment	Immovable	Seatbelt

Each word will be used once.

1. To protect yourself from hazardous moving parts of power tools and equipment, always use a/n _____ when using the equipment.

2. To avoid being caught in a/n _____, do not work in an unprotected trench that is _____ deep or more.

3. Wear a/n _____, if required, to avoid being thrown from a vehicle and then crushed by the vehicle as it tips over.

4. Make sure all loads carried by equipment are stable and _____.

5. Never place yourself between moving materials and a/n _____ structure, vehicle, or _____ materials.

6. Your employer must train you on how to use any provided _____ safely.

7. A competent person is capable of _____ hazards in the work environment and is authorized to take _____ measures.

Construction Focus Four: Caught-In or -Between Hazards Lesson Test

NAME: _____   DATE: ___/___/___

1. Caught in or -between hazards are related with excavations [trenches]; therefore, the hazard considered to be the greatest risk is:
   a. Cave-ins
   b. Severing of underground utilities
   c. Equipment falling into trenches

2. One who is capable of identifying existing and predictable hazards in the surroundings, or working conditions which are unsanitary, hazardous, or dangerous to employees, and who has authorization to take prompt corrective measures to eliminate them is a/n _____:
   a. Competent person
   b. OSHA Compliance Officer
   c. Qualified person

3. To protect against caught-in or –between hazards, a worker should not only avoid wearing loose clothing or jewelry, but also a worker should avoid:
   a. Operating equipment/machinery while wearing a seatbelt
   b. Working with equipment/machinery that has not been locked-out
   c. Using equipment/machinery that is guarded

4. Providing worker training on the safe use of the equipment being operated is the responsibility of the:
   a. Employer
   b. Worker
   c. State OSHA consultation

5. Workers should not work in an unprotected trench that is 5 feet deep or more. The type of protection installed may be sloping or benching; trench box or shield; and _____.
   a. Stabilizing
   b. Steadying
   c. Shoring

6. To prevent being pinned between equipment or other objects, workers should avoid _____.
   a. Using a trench box or shield during excavation work
   b. Placing themselves between moving vehicles and an immovable structure, vehicle, or staked materials
   c. Removing a safety guard when a tool such as, a circular saw or power drill, is being used.

Cranes

OSHA® FactSheet

Subpart CC – Cranes and Derricks in Construction: Assembly/Disassembly

This fact sheet explains the assembly and disassembly requirements of subpart CC – Cranes and Derricks in Construction, as specified in 29 CFR 1926.1403-1926.1406 and 192.1412. These provisions are effective November 8, 2010.

Procedures

Under this standard, employers must comply with all manufacturer prohibitions regarding assembly and disassembly. However, the standard generally allows employers to choose between the manufacturer's procedures or their own (see exception below for synthetic slings procedures). Employer procedures must be developed by a "qualified person" and must satisfy a number of specified requirements, such as providing adequate support and stability for all parts of the equipment, and positioning employees involved to minimize exposure to any unintended movement or collapse.

Assembly/Disassembly responsibilities

- The rule requires the work to be directed by an A/D (Assembly/Disassembly) director. The A/D director must meet the criteria for both a "competent person" and a "qualified person," which are defined terms in this rule, or must be a "competent person" assisted by a "qualified person."
- The A/D director must understand the applicable procedures.
- The A/D director must review the procedures immediately prior to beginning work unless he or she understands the procedures and has used them before for that equipment type and configuration.
- The A/D director must ensure that each member of the crew understands his or her tasks, the hazards of the tasks, and any hazardous positions or locations to avoid.
- The A/D director must verify all capacities of any equipment used, including rigging, lifting lugs, etc.
- The A/D director must also address hazards associated with the operation, including 12 specified areas of concern: site and ground conditions, blocking material, proper location of blocking, verifying assist crane loads, boom & jib pick points, center of gravity, stability upon pin removal, snagging, struck by counterweights, boom hoist brake failure, loss of backward stability, and wind speed and weather.

Inspection

- Upon completion of assembly, but before use, the equipment must be inspected by a "qualified person" to ensure that it is configured in accordance with the manufacturer equipment criteria. If these criteria are unavailable, the employer's "qualified person," with the assistance of a registered professional engineer if necessary, must develop the appropriate configuration criteria and ensure that these criteria are met.

For more complete information:

OSHA® Occupational Safety and Health Administration

U.S. Department of Labor
www.osha.gov
(800) 321-OSHA

Page 1 of 2

Assembly/Disassembly, continued.

General requirements

- A crew member who moves out of the operator's view to a location where the crew member could be injured by movement of the equipment (or load) MUST inform the operator before going to that location. The operator must not move the equipment until that crew member informs the operator that he or she has relocated to a safe position.
- Employees must never be under the boom or jib when pins (or similar devices) are being removed, unless it is required by site constraints and the A/D director has implemented procedures that minimize the risk of unintended movement and the duration and extent of exposure under the boom.
- Component weights must be readily available for all components to be assembled.
- All rigging must be done by a "qualified rigger."
- Pins may not be removed during disassembly when the pendants are in tension.
- Booms supported only by cantilevering must not exceed manufacturer limitations or RPE limitations, as applicable.
- Component selection and equipment configuration that affects the capacity or safe operation of the equipment must be in accordance with manufacturer requirements and limits or RPE requirements and limits, as applicable.

Synthetic slings

- The employer must follow manufacturer procedures when using synthetic slings during assembly or disassembly rigging

(even when the employer has developed its own A/D procedure as an alternative to the manufacturer's other procedures.)
- Synthetic slings must be protected from abrasive, sharp or acute edges, and configurations that might reduce the sling's rated capacity.

Outriggers and stabilizers

When outriggers or stabilizers are used or are necessary in light of the load to be handled and the operating radius:

- Outriggers and stabilizers must be fully extended or, if permitted by manufacturer procedures, deployed as specified in the load chart.
- Outriggers must be set to remove equipment weight from the wheels, except for locomotive cranes.
- Outrigger floats, if used, must be attached to the outriggers; stabilizer floats, if used, must be attached to the stabilizers.
- Each outrigger or stabilizer must be visible to the operator or to a signal person during extension and setting.
- Outrigger and stabilizer blocking must be placed under the float/pad of the jack or, if there is no jack, under the outer bearing surface of the outrigger or stabilizer beam. Blocking must also be sufficient to sustain the loads and maintain stability and must be properly placed.

Tower cranes

- Tower cranes are subject to additional requirements for erecting, climbing and dismantling, including a pre-erection inspection (29 CFR 1926.1435).

This is one in a series of informational fact sheets highlighting OSHA programs, policies or standards. It does not impose any new compliance requirements. For a comprehensive list of compliance requirements of OSHA standards or regulations, refer to Title 29 of the Code of Federal Regulations. This information will be made available to sensory impaired individuals upon request. The voice phone is (202) 693-1999; teletypewriter (TTY) number: (877) 889-5627.

For more complete information:

OSHA Occupational Safety and Health Administration

U.S. Department of Labor
www.osha.gov
(800) 321-OSHA

Page 2 of 2

Subpart CC – Cranes and Derricks in Construction: Wire Rope – Inspection

This fact sheet describes the inspection requirements of subpart CC – Cranes and Derricks in Construction, as specified in 29 CFR 1926.1413. These provisions are effective November 8, 2010. This document is intended to assist wire rope inspectors and supervisors.

Inspection Trigger	Inspection Details	Performed by	Documentation
Each shift	See list below, visual inspection must begin prior to each shift in which the equipment is used.	Competent Person	Not required
Monthly	See details below.	Competent Person	Required. Must be signed by the person who conducted the inspection and retained for a minimum of 3 months.
Annual	See details below.	Qualified Person	Required. Must be signed by the person who conducted the inspection and retained for a minimum of 12 months.

- The annual/comprehensive and monthly inspections must be documented according to 1926.1412(f)(7) and 1916.1412(e)(3), respectively.
- Rope lubricants of the type that hinder inspection must not be used.
- All documents produced under this section must be available, during the applicable document retention period, to all persons who conduct inspections under this section.

Shift Inspection

Shift inspections are visual inspections that a competent person must begin prior to each shift during which the equipment is used. Shift inspections do not require untwisting (opening) of wire ropes or booming down. The inspection must consist of observation of wire ropes (running and standing) that are likely to be in use during the shift for apparent deficiencies, including the following:

Apparent Deficiencies – Category I	Removal from Service Criteria
• Significant distortion of the wire rope structure such as kinking, crushing, unstranding, birdcaging, signs of core failure, or steel core protrusion between the outer strands. • Significant corrosion. • Electric arc damage (from a source other than power lines) or heat damage. • Improperly applied end connections. • Significantly corroded, cracked, bent, or worn end connections (such as from severe service).	If a Category I deficiency is identified, the competent person must immediately determine whether it constitutes a safety hazard. If the deficiency is determined to be a safety hazard, all operations involving use of the wire rope in question must be prohibited until: • The wire rope is replaced. (See 1926.1417), or • If the deficiency is localized, the problem is corrected by severing the wire rope in two; the undamaged portion may continue to be used. Joining lengths of wire rope by splicing is prohibited. If a rope is shortened under this paragraph, the employer must ensure that the drum will still have two wraps of wire when the load and/or boom is in its lowest position.

Apparent Deficiencies – Category II	Removal from Service Criteria

• Visible broken wires:
  ◦ In running wire ropes: six randomly distributed broken wires in one rope lay or three broken wires in one strand in one rope lay, where a rope lay is the length along the rope in which one strand makes a complete revolution around the rope.
  ◦ In rotation-resistant ropes: two randomly distributed broken wires in six rope diameters or four randomly distributed broken wires in 30 rope diameters.
  ◦ In pendants or standing wire ropes: more than two broken wires in one rope lay located in rope beyond end connections and/or more than one broken wire in a rope lay located at an end connection.
• A diameter reduction of more than 5% from nominal diameter.
	If a Category II deficiency is identified, operations involving use of the wire rope in question must be prohibited until:
	• Employer complies with the wire rope manufacturer's established criterion for removal from service, or with a different criterion that the wire rope manufacturer has approved in writing for that specific wire rope. (See 1926.1417).
	• The wire rope is replaced. (See 1926.1417), or
	• If the deficiency is localized, the problem is corrected by severing the wire rope in two; the undamaged portion may continue to be used. Joining lengths of wire rope by splicing is prohibited. If a rope is shortened under this paragraph, the employer must ensure that the drum will still have two wraps of wire when the load and/or boom is in its lowest position.

Apparent Deficiencies – Category III	Removal from Service Criteria
• In rotation-resistant wire rope, core protrusion or other distortion indicating core failure. • Prior electrical contact with a power line. • A broken strand.	If a Category III deficiency is identified, operations involving use of the wire rope in question must be prohibited until: • The wire rope is replaced. (See 1926.1417), or • If the deficiency (other than power line contact) is localized, the problem is corrected by severing the wire rope in two; the undamaged portion may continue to be used. Joining lengths of wire rope by splicing is prohibited. Repair of wire rope that contacted an energized power line is also prohibited. If a rope is shortened under this paragraph, the employer must ensure that the drum will still have two wraps of wire when the load and/or boom is in its lowest position.

Where a wire rope is required to be removed from service under this section, either the equipment (as a whole), or the hoist with that wire rope must be tagged-out, in accord with 1926.1417(f)(1), until the wire rope is repaired or replaced.

Critical Review Items

Particular attention must be given to all of the following:

• Rotation-resistant wire rope in use.
• Wire rope being used for boom hoists and luffing hoists, particularly at reverse bends.
• Wire rope at flange points, crossover points, and repetitive pickup points on drums.
• Wire rope at or near terminal ends.
• Wire rope in contact with saddles, equalizer sheaves or other sheaves where rope travel is limited.

Monthly Inspection

Each month an inspection must be conducted as stated under "Shift Inspection" above.

In addition to the criteria for shift inspection, monthly inspections require that:

• The inspection must include any deficiencies that the qualified person who conducts the annual inspection determines under 1926.1413(c)(3)(ii) must be monitored.
• Wire ropes on equipment must not be used until an inspection under this paragraph demonstrates that no corrective action under 1926.1413(a)(4) is required.
• The inspection must be documented according to 1926.1412(e)(3) (monthly inspection documentation).

Annual/Comprehensive Inspection

At least every 12 months, wire ropes in use on equipment must be inspected by a qualified person as stated under "Shift Inspection" above.

In addition to the criteria for shift inspection, annual inspections require that –

- The inspection must be complete and thorough, covering the surface of the entire length of the wire ropes, with particular attention given to all of the following:
  - Critical review items from 1926.1413(a)(3)–(see "Critical Review Items" above).
  - Those sections that are normally hidden during shift and monthly inspections.
  - Wire rope subject to reverse bends.
  - Wire rope passing over sheaves.

Exception

In the event an annual inspection under 1926.1413(c)(2) is not feasible due to existing set-up and configuration of the equipment (such as where an assist crane is needed) or due to site conditions (such as a dense urban setting), such inspections must be conducted as soon as it becomes feasible, but no longer than an additional 6 months for running ropes and, for standing ropes, at the time of disassembly.

- If a deficiency is determined to constitute a safety hazard, operations involving use of the wire rope in question must be prohibited until:
  - The wire rope is replaced (see 1926.1417), or
  - If the deficiency is localized, the problem is corrected by severing the wire rope in two; the undamaged portion may continue to be used. Joining wire rope by splicing is prohibited. If a rope is shortened under this paragraph, the employer must ensure that the drum will still have two wraps of wire when the load and/or boom is in its lowest position.
- If a deficiency is identified and the qualified person determines that, though not presently a safety hazard, the deficiency needs to be monitored, the employer must ensure that the deficiency is checked in the monthly inspections.

Additionally

- The inspection must be documented according to 1926.1412(f)(7).
- Rope lubricants of the type that hinder inspection must not be used.
- All documents produced under this section must be available, during the applicable document retention period, to all persons who conduct inspections under this section.

Name: _____   Date: _____

Knowledge Check: Cranes

1. Nearly 45% of crane accidents are the result of the boom or crane making contact with ___.
   a. other cranes
   b. work zone barricades
   c. energized power lines
   d. workers on the ground

2. Before beginning equipment operations, the employer must ___.
   a. identify the work zone and determine proximity to power lines
   b. notify utility company of lift and estimate voltage of power lines
   c. locate the fall zone and test load by lifting it at least 20 feet off the ground
   d. remove hazard area barriers and observe weather conditions

3. A broken window that distorts the operator's visibility of the task is acceptable for operation.
   a. True
   b. False

4. Which of the following must be readily available to the crane operator for use at all times?
   a. Load charts and recommended operating speeds
   b. Special hazard warnings
   c. Instructions and operator's manual
   d. All of the above

5. Who is responsible for inspecting all machinery and equipment prior to each use and during use, to make sure it is in safe operating condition.
   a. Certified person
   b. Qualified person
   c. Proficient person
   d. Competent person

Excavations

OSHA® FactSheet

Trenching and Excavation Safety

Two workers are killed every month in trench collapses. The employer must provide a workplace free of recognized hazards that may cause serious injury or death. The employer must comply with the trenching and excavation requirements of 29 CFR 1926.651 and 1926.652 or comparable OSHA-approved state plan requirements.

An excavation is any man-made cut, cavity, trench, or depression in an earth surface formed by earth removal.

Trench (Trench excavation) means a narrow excavation (in relation to its length) made below the surface of the ground. In general, the depth is greater than the width, but the width of a trench (measured at the bottom) is not greater than 15 feet (4.6 meters).

Dangers of Trenching and Excavation

Cave-ins pose the greatest risk and are much more likely than other excavation-related accidents to result in worker fatalities. Other potential hazards include falls, falling loads, hazardous atmospheres, and incidents involving mobile equipment. One cubic yard of soil can weigh as much as a car. An unprotected trench is an early grave. Do not enter an unprotected trench.

Trench Safety Measures

Trenches 5 feet (1.5 meters) deep or greater require a protective system unless the excavation is made entirely in stable rock. If less than 5 feet deep, a competent person may determine that a protective system is not required.

Trenches 20 feet (6.1 meters) deep or greater require that the protective system be designed by a registered professional engineer or be based on tabulated data prepared and/or approved by a registered professional engineer in accordance with 1926.652(b) and (c).

Competent Person

OSHA standards require that employers inspect trenches daily and as conditions change by a competent person before worker entry to ensure elimination of excavation hazards. A competent person is an individual who is capable of identifying existing and predictable hazards or working conditions that are hazardous, unsanitary, or dangerous to workers, soil types and protective systems required, and who is authorized to take prompt corrective measures to eliminate these hazards and conditions.

Access and Egress

OSHA standards require safe access and egress to all excavations, including ladders, steps, ramps, or other safe means of exit for employees working in trench excavations 4 feet (1.22 meters) or deeper. These devices must be located within 25 feet (7.6 meters) of all workers.

General Trenching and Excavation Rules

- Keep heavy equipment away from trench edges.
- Identify other sources that might affect trench stability.
- Keep excavated soil (spoils) and other materials at least 2 feet (0.6 meters) from trench edges.
- Know where underground utilities are located before digging.
- Test for atmospheric hazards such as low oxygen, hazardous fumes and toxic gases when > 4 feet deep.
- Inspect trenches at the start of each shift.
- Inspect trenches following a rainstorm or other water intrusion.
- Do not work under suspended or raised loads and materials.
- Inspect trenches after any occurrence that could have changed conditions in the trench.
- Ensure that personnel wear high visibility or other suitable clothing when exposed to vehicular traffic.

Protective Systems

There are different types of protective systems.

Benching means a method of protecting workers from cave-ins by excavating the sides of an excavation to form one or a series of horizontal levels or steps, usually with vertical or near-vertical surfaces between levels. *Benching cannot be done in Type C soil.*

Sloping involves cutting back the trench wall at an angle inclined away from the excavation.

Shoring requires installing aluminum hydraulic or other types of supports to prevent soil movement and cave-ins.

Shielding protects workers by using trench boxes or other types of supports to prevent soil cave-ins. Designing a protective system can be complex because you must consider many factors: soil classification, depth of cut, water content of soil, changes caused by weather or climate, surcharge loads (e.g., spoil, other materials to be used in the trench) and other operations in the vicinity.

Additional Information

Visit OSHA's Safety and Health Topics web page on trenching and excavation at
www.osha.gov/SLTC/trenchingexcavation/index.html
www.osha.gov/dcsp/statestandard.html

This is one in a series of informational fact sheets highlighting OSHA programs, policies or standards. It does not impose any new compliance requirements. For a comprehensive list of compliance requirements of OSHA standards or regulations, refer to Title 29 of the Code of Federal Regulations. This information will be made available to sensory-impaired individuals upon request. The voice phone is (202) 693-1999; teletypewriter (TTY) number: (877) 889-5627.

For assistance, contact us. We can help. It's confidential.

U.S. Department of Labor
www.osha.gov   (800) 321-OSHA (6742)

DOC FS-3476 9/2011

Name: _____   Date: _____

Knowledge Check: Excavations

1. What is the minimum distance that excavation materials, tools, and other supplies be kept back from the excavation's edge?
    a. 1 foot
    b. 2 feet
    c. 7.5 feet
    d. 25 feet

2. At what depth must a ladder, ramp, steps, or runway be present for quick worker exit?
    a. 4 feet
    b. 5 feet
    c. 10 feet
    d. It is never required

3. What is the greatest hazard facing a worker while working in a trench?
    a. Hazardous atmospheres
    b. Falls
    c. Cave-ins
    d. Falling objects

4. Unless made in entirely stable rock, at what depth is a protective system required for a trench?
    a. Any depth if the competent person says so
    b. 5 feet and greater
    c. Only at depths greater than 10 feet
    d. Both a and b

Materials handling

Worker Safety Series
Warehousing

Think Safety

- More than 145,000 people work in over 7,000 warehouses.
- The fatal injury rate for the warehousing industry is higher than the national average for all industries.
- Potential hazards for workers in warehousing:
  o Unsafe use of forklifts;
  o Improper stacking of products;
  o Failure to use proper personal protective equipment;
  o Failure to follow proper lockout/tagout procedures;
  o Inadequate fire safety provisions; or
  o Repetitive motion injuries.

Think Safety Checklists

The following checklists may help you take steps to avoid hazards that cause injuries, illnesses and fatalities. As always, be cautious and seek help if you are concerned about a potential hazard.

General Safety

- Exposed or open loading dock doors and other areas that employees could fall 4 feet or more or walk off should be chained off, roped off or otherwise blocked.
- Floors and aisles are clear of clutter, electrical cords, hoses, spills and other hazards that could cause employees to slip, trip or fall.
- Proper work practices are factored into determining the time requirements for an employee to perform a task.
- Employees performing physical work have adequate periodic rest breaks to avoid fatigue levels that could result in greater risk of accidents and reduced quality of work.
- Newly-hired employees receive general ergonomics training and task-specific training.
- The warehouse is well ventilated.
- Employees are instructed on how to avoid heat stress in hot, humid environments.
- Employees are instructed on how to work in cold environments.
- The facility has lockout/tagout procedures.

Materials Handling Safety

- There are appropriately marked and sufficiently safe clearances for aisles and at loading docks or passageways where mechanical handling equipment is used.
- Loose/unboxed materials which might fall from a pile are properly stacked by blocking, interlocking or limiting the height of the pile to prevent falling hazards.

- Bags, containers, bundles, etc. are stored in tiers that are stacked, blocked, interlocked and limited in height so that they are stable and secure to prevent sliding or collapse.
- Storage areas are kept free from accumulation of materials that could lead to tripping, fire, explosion or pest infestations.
- Excessive vegetation is removed from building entrances, work or traffic areas to prevent possible trip or fall hazards due to visual obstructions.
- Derail and/or bumper blocks are provided on spur railroad tracks where a rolling car could contact other cars being worked on and at entrances to buildings, work or traffic areas.
- Covers and/or guardrails are provided to protect personnel from the hazards of stair openings in floors, meter or equipment pits and similar hazards.
- Personnel use proper lifting techniques.
- Elevators and hoists for lifting materials/ containers are properly used with adequate safe clearances, no obstructions, appropriate signals and directional warning signs.

Hazard Communication Safety

- All hazardous materials containers are properly labeled, indicating the chemical's identity, the manufacturer's name and address, and appropriate hazard warnings.
- There is an updated list of hazardous chemicals.
- The facility has a written program that covers hazard determination, including Material Safety Data Sheets (MSDSs), labeling and training.
- There is a system to check that each incoming chemical is accompanied by a MSDS.
- All employees are trained in the requirements of the hazard communication standard, the chemical hazards to which they are exposed, how to read and understand a MSDS and chemical labels, and on what precautions to take to prevent exposure.
- All employee training is documented.
- All outside contractors are given a complete list of chemical products, hazards and precautions.
- Procedures have been established to maintain and evaluate the effectiveness of the current program.
- Employees use proper personal protective equipment when handling chemicals.
- All chemicals are stored according to the manufacturer's recommendations and local or national fire codes.

Forklift Safety

- Powered industrial trucks (forklifts) meet the design and construction requirements established in American National Standard for Powered Industrial Trucks, Part II ANSI B56.1-1969.
- Written approval from the truck manufacturer has been obtained for any modifications or additions that affect the capacity and safe operation of the vehicle.
- Capacity, operation and maintenance instruction plates, tags or decals are changed to specify any modifications or additions to the vehicle.
- Nameplates and markings are in place and maintained in a legible condition.
- Forklifts that are used in hazardous locations are appropriately marked/approved for such use.
- Battery charging is conducted only in designated areas.
- Appropriate facilities are provided for flushing and neutralizing spilled electrolytes, for fire extinguishing, for protecting charging apparatus from damage by trucks and for adequate ventilation to disperse fumes from gassing batteries.
- Conveyors, overhead hoists or equivalent materials handling equipment are provided for handling batteries.
- Reinstalled batteries are properly positioned and secured.

- Carboy tilters or siphons are used for handling electrolytes.
- Forklifts are properly positioned and brakes applied before workers start to change or charge batteries.
- Vent caps are properly functioning.
- Precautions are taken to prevent smoking, open flames, sparks or electric arcs in battery charging areas and during storage/changing of propane fuel tanks.
- Tools and other metallic objects are kept away from the top of uncovered batteries.
- Concentrations of noxious gases and fumes are kept below acceptable levels.
- Forklift operators are competent to operate a vehicle safely as demonstrated by successful completion of training and evaluation conducted and certified by persons with the knowledge, training and experience to train operators and evaluate their performance.
- The training program content includes all truck-related topics, workplace related topics and the requirements of 29 CFR 1910.178 for safe truck operation.
- Refresher training and evaluation is conducted whenever an operator has been observed operating the vehicle in an unsafe manner or has been involved in an accident or a near-miss incident.
- Refresher training and evaluation is conducted whenever an operator is assigned to drive a different type of truck or whenever a condition in the workplace changes in a manner that could affect safe operation of the truck.
- Evaluations of each operator's performance are conducted at least once every three years.
- Load engaging means are fully lowered, with controls neutralized, power shut off and brakes set when a forklift is left unattended.
- Operators maintain a safe distance from the edge of ramps or platforms while using forklifts on any elevated dock, platform or freight car.
- There is sufficient headroom for the forklift and operator under overhead installations, lights, pipes, sprinkler systems, etc.
- Overhead guards are provided in good condition to protect forklift operators from falling objects.
- Operators observe all traffic regulations, including authorized plant speed limits.
- Drivers are required to look in the direction of and keep a clear view of the path of travel.
- Operators run their trucks at a speed that will permit the vehicle to stop in a safe manner.
- Dock boards (bridge plates) are properly secured when loading or unloading from dock to truck.
- Stunt driving and horseplay are prohibited.
- All loads are stable, safely arranged and fit within the rated capacity of the truck.
- Operators fill fuel tanks only when the engine is not running.
- Replacement parts of trucks are equivalent in terms of safety with those used in the original design.
- Trucks are examined for safety before being placed into service and unsafe or defective trucks are removed from service.

Name: _____   Date: _____

Knowledge Check: Materials Handling, Storage, Use, and Disposal

1. How old do you have to be to operate a forklift, regardless of training?
   a. 16 years old
   b. 18 years old
   c. 21 years old
   d. 25 years old

2. One good way to prevent materials handling hazards is to _____.
   a. refuse to allow personnel to ride equipment without a seat and seatbelt
   b. report all damaged equipment immediately
   c. operate within manufacturer's specifications
   d. All of these

3. Which of the following is a method for eliminating or reducing crane operation hazards?
   a. Operators should know how much they are lifting as well as the rated capacity of the crane.
   b. A competent person should visually inspect the crane once a year.
   c. Never exceed the load limit by more than 10%.
   d. All of these.

4. Employers must comply with OSHA standards related to materials handling, including training and _____.
   a. equipment
   b. operations
   c. inspection
   d. All of these

Scaffolds

OSHA® FactSheet

Tube and Coupler Scaffolds — Erection and Use

Workers building scaffolds risk serious injury from falls and tip-overs, being struck by falling tools and other hazards, and electrocution from energized power lines. Before starting any scaffold project, the employer should conduct a hazard assessment to ensure the safety of workers.

A tube and coupler scaffold has a platform(s) supported by tubing, and is erected with coupling devices connecting uprights, braces, bearers, and runners (see Fig. 1). Due to their strength, these scaffolds are frequently used where heavy loads need to be carried, or where multiple platforms must reach several stories high. These scaffolds can be assembled in multiple directions, making them the preferred option for work surfaces with irregular dimensions and/or contours.

When Erecting a Scaffold

- Use footings that are level, sound, rigid and capable of supporting the load without settlement or displacement.
- Plumb and brace poles, legs, posts, frames, and uprights to prevent swaying and displacement.
- Position the first level of bracing as close to the base as possible.
- Plumb and level the scaffold as it is being erected.
- Fasten all couplers and/or connections securely before assembling the next level.
- Install guys, ties, and braces according to the manufacturer's recommendations.
- Do not intermix scaffold components from different manufacturers, unless you can do so while maintaining the scaffold's structural integrity.
- When platform units are abutted together to create a long platform, each abutted end must rest on a separate support surface.
- Once erected, provide toeboards on all railed sides to prevent falling object hazards.

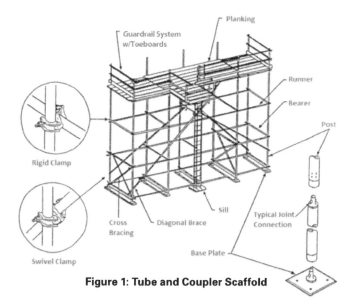

Figure 1: Tube and Coupler Scaffold

When Using a Scaffold

- Make sure that a competent person inspects the scaffold before each work shift.
- If during the inspection a defect or damage to the scaffold is discovered, the scaffold must be tagged out and not used until repairs are made. Attach tags at the access point to the scaffold.

One common tagging system uses the following tags:

Red tag indicates: unsafe, do not use.
Green tag indicates: ready to use.

- Use scaffolds according to the manufacturer's instructions.
- Never load a scaffold beyond its maximum intended load or rated capacity.
- Do not use makeshift methods to increase the working height of the scaffold platform, such as with ladders, buckets or blocks.

120

- Employees must not work on platforms covered with snow, ice, or other slippery material.
- The employer must provide suitable access to and between scaffolds, such as portable ladders, hook-on ladders, attachable ladders and stairway-type ladders.

When Dismantling a Scaffold

Check to ensure that the scaffold has not been structurally altered in a way which would make it unsafe. Before beginning dismantling procedures, reconstruct and/or stabilize the scaffold as necessary.

Training Workers

Only trained and authorized persons should be allowed to use a scaffold. This training must be provided by a qualified person who understands the hazards associated with the type of scaffold being used and who knows the procedures to control or minimize those hazards. Training must include how to safely:

- Use the scaffold, handle materials on the scaffold and determine the maximum load limits when handling materials.
- Recognize and avoid scaffolding hazards such as electric shock, falls from heights, and being hit by falling objects.
- Erect, maintain and disassemble fall and falling object protection systems.

Erectors and dismantlers of tube and coupler scaffolds are at particular risk because their work starts before ladders, guardrails and platforms are completely installed. These workers must also be trained to:

- Recognize scaffold hazards.
- Properly erect, move, operate, repair, inspect, maintain and disassemble the scaffold;
- Identify the maximum load-carrying capacity and intended use of the scaffold.

Employers should train workers on the following safety factors:

- The shape and structure of the building to be scaffolded.

- Distinctive site conditions and any special features of the building structure in relation to the scaffold (i.e., overhead electric power lines or storage tanks). Also consider the proximity and condition of surrounding buildings.
- Weather and environmental conditions.
- Fall protection requirements for workers using scaffolds, such as guardrail systems or personal fall arrest systems.
- The type and amount of scaffold equipment needed to access all areas to be worked on.
- Proper storage and transporting of scaffolding components, materials and equipment.
- How to access the scaffold, (i.e., via ladders, stair rail systems, etc.).

Workers building scaffolds risk serious injury from falls and tip-overs, being struck by falling tools and other hazards, and electrocution from energized power lines.

To avoid scaffold hazards, employers must:

- Ensure that a competent person supervises and directs workers erecting, moving, dismantling, or altering a scaffold.
- Provide a safe means of access for each worker erecting or dismantling the scaffold. As early as possible, install hook-on or attachable ladders.
- Ensure that workers do not climb diagonal braces to reach the scaffold platform.
- Provide fall protection for workers erecting or dismantling the scaffold.
- Secure scaffolds to the structure during erection and dismantling.

For more information on scaffolding, see OSHA's Safety and Health Topics page at www.osha.gov/SLTC/scaffolding.

Contact OSHA

For more information, to report an emergency, fatality or catastrophe, to order publications, to file a confidential complaint, or to request OSHA's free on-site consultation service, contact your nearest OSHA office, visit www.osha.gov, or call OSHA at 1-800-321-OSHA (6742), TTY 1-877-889-5627.

Worker Rights

Workers have the right to:

- Working conditions that do not pose a risk of serious harm.
- Receive information and training (in a language and vocabulary the worker understands) about workplace hazards, methods to prevent them, and the OSHA standards that apply to their workplace.
- Review records of work-related injuries and illnesses.

- File a complaint asking OSHA to inspect their workplace if they believe there is a serious hazard or that their employer is not following OSHA's rules. OSHA will keep all identities confidential.
- Exercise their rights under the law without retaliation, including reporting an injury or raising health and safety concerns with their employer or OSHA. If a worker has been retaliated against for using their rights, they must file a complaint with OSHA as soon as possible, but no later than 30 days.

For more information, see OSHA's Workers page.

This is one in a series of informational fact sheets highlighting OSHA programs, policies or standards. It does not impose any new compliance requirements. For a comprehensive list of compliance requirements of OSHA standards or regulations, refer to Title 29 of the Code of Federal Regulations. This information will be made available to sensory-impaired individuals upon request. The voice phone is (202) 693-1999; teletypewriter (TTY) number: 1-877-889-5627.

For assistance, contact us. We can help. It's confidential.

Occupational Safety and Health Administration

www.osha.gov (800) 321-OSHA (6742)

U.S. Department of Labor

DOC FS-3759 11/2014

Name: _____   Date: _____

Knowledge Check: Scaffolds

1. Who trains employees that work on scaffolds?
    a. Employees do not need training
    b. Employees are responsible for their own training
    c. Fellow employees who have experience
    d. Employer-designated competent person

2. Scaffold plans must be developed by a _____.
    a. competent person
    b. construction site manager
    c. qualified person
    d. experience scaffold worker

3. Which of the following is NOT an example of proper access?
    a. Ladders
    b. Crossbraces
    c. Stair towers
    d. Walkways

Stairways and ladders

OSHA FactSheet

Reducing Falls in Construction: Safe Use of Extension Ladders

Workers who use extension ladders risk permanent injury or death from falls and electrocutions. These hazards can be eliminated or substantially reduced by following good safety practices. This fact sheet examines some of the hazards workers may encounter while working on **extension ladders** and explains what employers and workers can do to reduce injuries. OSHA's requirements for extension ladders are in Subpart X—Stairways and Ladders of OSHA's Construction standards.

What is an Extension Ladder?

Also known as "portable ladders," extension ladders usually have two sections that operate in brackets or guides allowing for adjustable lengths. (See Figure 1, below.) Because extension ladders are not self-supporting they require a stable structure that can withstand the intended load.

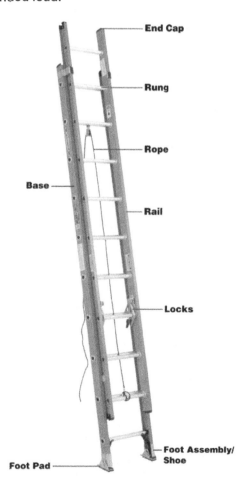

Figure 1: Extension Ladder

- End Cap
- Rung
- Rope
- Base
- Rail
- Locks
- Foot Assembly/Shoe
- Foot Pad

PLAN Ahead to Get the Job Done Safely.

- Use a ladder that can sustain at least four times the maximum intended load, except that each extra-heavy duty type 1A metal or plastic ladder shall sustain at least 3.3 times the maximum intended load. Also acceptable are ladders that meet the requirements set forth in Appendix A of Subpart X. Follow the manufacturer's instructions and labels on the ladder. To determine the correct ladder, consider your weight plus the weight of your load. Do not exceed the load rating and always include the weight of all tools, materials and equipment.
- A competent person must visually inspect all extension ladders before use for any defects such as: missing rungs, bolts, cleats, screws and loose components. Where a ladder has these or other defects, it must be immediately marked as defective or tagged with "Do Not Use" or similar language.
- Allow sufficient room to step off the ladder safely. Keep the area around the bottom and the top of the ladder clear of equipment, materials and tools. If access is obstructed, secure the top of the ladder to a rigid support that will not deflect, and add a grasping device to allow workers safe access.
- Set the ladder at the proper angle. When a ladder is leaned against a wall, the bottom of the ladder should be one-quarter of the ladder's working length away from the wall. For access to an elevated work surface, extend the top of the ladder three feet above that surface or secure the ladder at its top.
- Before starting work, survey the area for potential hazards, such as energized overhead power lines. Ladders shall have

126

nonconductive side rails if they are used where the worker or the ladder could contact exposed energized electrical equipment. Keep all ladders and other tools at least 10 feet away from any power lines.

- Set the base of the ladder so that the bottom sits securely and so both side rails are evenly supported. The ladder rails should be square to the structure against which it is leaning with both footpads placed securely on a stable and level surface.
- Secure the ladder's dogs or pawls before climbing.
- When using a ladder in a high-activity area, secure it to prevent movement and use a barrier to redirect workers and equipment. If the ladder is placed in front of a door, always block off the door.

Figure 2: Ladder extending three feet above the landing area.

PROVIDE the Right Extension Ladder for the Job with the Proper Load Capacity.

Select a ladder based on the expected load capacity (duty rating), the type of work to be done and the correct height. There are five categories of ladder duty ratings.

Type	Duty Rating	Use	Load
IAA*	Special Duty	Rugged	375 lbs.
IA	Extra Duty	Industrial	300 lbs.
I	Heavy Duty	Industrial	250 lbs.
II	Medium Duty	Commercial	225 lbs.
III	Light Duty	Household	200 lbs.

Source for Types IA, I, II, III: Subpart X—Stairways and Ladders, Appendix A (American National Standards Institute (ANSI)) 14.1, 14.2, 14.5 (1982)) of OSHA's Construction standards. Source for Type IAA: ANSI 14.1, 14.2, 14.5 (2009), which are non-mandatory guidelines.

TRAIN Workers to Use Extension Ladders Safely.

Employers must train each worker to recognize and minimize ladder-related hazards.

PLAN. PROVIDE. TRAIN.

Three simple steps to prevent falls.

Safe Ladder Use—DO:

- Maintain a 3-point contact (two hands and a foot, or two feet and a hand) when climbing/descending a ladder.
- Face the ladder when climbing up or descending.
- Keep the body inside the side rails.
- Use extra care when getting on or off the ladder at the top or bottom. Avoid tipping the ladder over sideways or causing the ladder base to slide out.
- Carry tools in a tool belt or raise tools up using a hand line. Never carry tools in your hands while climbing up/down a ladder.
- Extend the top of the ladder three feet above the landing. (See Figure 2.)
- Keep ladders free of any slippery materials.

Safe Ladder Use—DO NOT:

- Place a ladder on boxes, barrels, or unstable bases.
- Use a ladder on soft ground or unstable footing.
- Exceed the ladder's maximum load rating.
- Tie two ladders together to make them longer.
- Ignore nearby overhead power lines.
- Move or shift a ladder with a person or equipment on the ladder.
- Lean out beyond the ladder's side rails.
- Use an extension ladder horizontally like a platform.

OSHA standard: **29 CFR 1926 Subpart X**—Stairways and Ladders

American National Standards Institute standard: **ANSI A14.1, A14.2, A14.5—Ladder Safety Requirements** *(Not an OSHA standard, included to be used as guidance to meet OSHA's requirements)*

Employers using extension ladders must follow the ladder requirements set forth in 29 CFR 1926 Subpart X. Per Appendix A to Subpart X of Part 1926—Ladders, ladders designed in accordance with the following ANSI standards will be considered in accordance with 29 CFR 1926.1053(a)(1): ANSI A14.1-1982—American National Standard for Ladders—Portable Wood—Safety Requirements, ANSI A14.2-1982—American National Standard for Ladders—Portable Metal—Safety Requirements, and ANSI A14.5-1982—American National Standard for Ladders—Portable Reinforced Plastic—Safety Requirements.

State plan guidance: States with OSHA-approved state plans may have additional requirements for avoiding falls from ladders. For more information on these requirements, please visit: www.osha.gov/dcsp/osp/statesstandards.html.

Most OSHA offices have compliance assistance specialists to help employers and workers comply with OSHA standards. For details call 1-800-321-OSHA (6742) or visit: www.osha.gov/htm/RAmap.html.

For assistance, contact us. We can help. It's confidential.

U.S. Department of Labor
www.osha.gov (800) 321-OSHA (6742)

DOC FS-3660 05/2013

128

OSHA® QUICK CARD™

Portable Ladder Safety

Falls from portable ladders (step, straight, combination and extension) are one of the leading causes of occupational fatalities and injuries.

• Read and follow all labels/markings on the ladder.

• Avoid electrical hazards! – Look for overhead power lines before handling a ladder. Avoid using a metal ladder near power lines or exposed energized electrical equipment.

• Always inspect the ladder prior to using it. If the ladder is damaged, it must be removed from service and tagged until repaired or discarded.

3-Point Contact

• Always maintain a 3-point (two hands and a foot, or two feet and a hand) contact on the ladder when climbing. Keep your body near the middle of the step and always face the ladder while climbing (see diagram).

• Only use ladders and appropriate accessories (ladder levelers, jacks or hooks) for their designed purposes.

• Ladders must be free of any slippery material on the rungs, steps or feet.

• Do not use a self-supporting ladder (e.g., step ladder) as a single ladder or in a partially closed position.

• Do not use the top step/rung of a ladder as a step/rung unless it was designed for that purpose.

(continued on reverse)

- Use a ladder only on a stable and level surface, unless it has been secured (top or bottom) to prevent displacement.

- Do not place a ladder on boxes, barrels or other unstable bases to obtain additional height.

- Do not move or shift a ladder while a person or equipment is on the ladder.

- An extension or straight ladder used to access an elevated surface must extend at least 3 feet above the point of support (see diagram). Do not stand on the three top rungs of a straight, single or extension ladder.

- The proper angle for setting up a ladder is to place its base a quarter of the working length of the ladder from the wall or other vertical surface (see diagram).

- A ladder placed in any location where it can be displaced by other work activities must be secured to prevent displacement or a barricade must be erected to keep traffic away from the ladder.

- Be sure that all locks on an extension ladder are properly engaged.

- Do not exceed the maximum load rating of a ladder. Be aware of the ladder's load rating and of the weight it is supporting, including the weight of any tools or equipment.

For more information:

OSHA® Occupational Safety and Health Administration

U.S. Department of Labor

www.osha.gov (800) 321-OSHA (6742)

OSHA 3246-10N-06

OSHA FactSheet

Reducing Falls in Construction: Safe Use of Stepladders

Workers who use ladders in construction risk permanent injury or death from falls and electrocutions. These hazards can be eliminated or substantially reduced by following good safety practices. This fact sheet examines some of the hazards workers may encounter while working on **stepladders** and explains what employers and workers can do to reduce injuries. OSHA's requirements for stepladders are in Subpart X—Stairways and Ladders of OSHA's Construction standards.

What is a Stepladder?

A **stepladder** is a portable, self-supporting, A-frame ladder. It has two front side rails and two rear side rails. Generally, there are steps mounted between the front side rails and bracing between the rear side rails. (See Figure 1, below.)

Top Cap

Top Step

Front Side Rails

Rear Side Rails

Step

Spreaders

Anti-Slip Safety Shoes/Feet

Figure 1: Stepladder

PLAN Ahead to Get the Job Done Safely.

A competent person must visually inspect stepladders for visible defects on a periodic basis and after any occurrence that could affect their safe use. Defects include, but are not limited to:

- Structural damage, split/bent side rails, broken or missing rungs/steps/cleats and missing or damaged safety devices.

- Grease, dirt or other contaminants that could cause slips or falls.
- Paint or stickers (except warning or safety labels) that could hide possible defects.

PROVIDE the Right Stepladder for the Job with the Proper Load Capacity.

- Use a ladder that can sustain at least four times the maximum intended load, except that each extra-heavy duty type 1A metal or plastic ladder shall sustain at least 3.3 times the maximum intended load. Also acceptable are ladders that meet the requirements set forth in Appendix A of Subpart X. Follow the manufacturer's instructions and labels on the ladder. To determine the correct ladder, consider your weight plus the weight of your load. Do not exceed the load rating and always include the weight of all tools, materials and equipment.

Type	Duty Rating	Use	Load
1AA	Special Duty	Rugged	375 lbs.
1A	Extra Heavy Duty	Industrial	300 lbs.
1	Heavy Duty	Industrial	250 lbs.
II	Medium Duty	Commercial	225 lbs.
III	Light Duty	Household	200 lbs.

Source for Types IA, I, II, III: Subpart X—Stairways and Ladders, Appendix A (American National Standards Institute (ANSI) 14.1, 14.2, 14.5 (1982)) of OSHA's Construction standards. Source for Type IAA: ANSI 14.1, 14.2, 14.5 (2009), which are non-mandatory guidelines.

TRAIN Workers to Use Stepladders Safely.

Employers must train each worker to recognize and minimize ladder-related hazards.

 **PLAN. PROVIDE. TRAIN.**
Three simple steps to prevent falls.

Common Stepladder Hazards

- Damaged stepladder
- Ladders on slippery or unstable surface
- Unlocked ladder spreaders
- Standing on the top step or top cap
- Loading ladder beyond rated load
- Ladders in high-traffic location
- Reaching outside ladder side rails
- Ladders in close proximity to electrical wiring/equipment

Safe Stepladder Use—DO:

Read and follow all the manufacturer's instructions and labels on the ladder.

- Look for overhead power lines before handling or climbing a ladder.
- Maintain a 3-point contact (two hands and a foot, or two feet and a hand) when climbing/descending a ladder.
- Stay near the middle of the ladder and face the ladder while climbing up/down.
- Use a barricade to keep traffic away from the ladder.
- Keep ladders free of any slippery materials.
- Only put ladders on a stable and level surface that is not slippery.

Safe Stepladder Use—DO NOT:

- Use ladders for a purpose other than that for which they were designed. For example, do not use a folded stepladder as a single ladder.
- Use a stepladder with spreaders unlocked.
- Use the top step or cap as a step.
- Place a ladder on boxes, barrels or other unstable bases.
- Move or shift a ladder with a person or equipment on the ladder.
- Use cross bracing on the rear of stepladders for climbing.
- Paint a ladder with opaque coatings.
- Use a damaged ladder.
- Leave tools/materials/equipment on stepladder.
- Use a stepladder horizontally like a platform.
- Use a metal stepladder near power lines or electrical equipment.

OSHA standard: 29 CFR 1926 Subpart X—Stairways and Ladders

American National Standards Institute standard: ANSI A14.1, A14.2, A14.5—Ladder Safety Requirements
(Not an OSHA standard, included to be used as guidance to meet OSHA's requirements)

Employers using stepladders must follow the ladder requirements set forth in 29 CFR 1926 Subpart X. Per Appendix A to Subpart X of Part 1926—Ladders, ladders designed in accordance with the following ANSI standards will be considered in accordance with 29 CFR 1926.1053(a)(1): ANSI A14.1-1982—American National Standard for Ladders-Portable Wood-Safety Requirements, ANSI A14.2-1982—American National Standard for Ladders—Portable Metal—Safety Requirements, and ANSI A14.5-1982—American National Standard for Ladders—Portable Reinforced Plastic—Safety Requirements.

State plan guidance: States with OSHA-approved state plans may have additional requirements for avoiding falls from ladders. For more information on these requirements, please visit: www.osha.gov/dcsp/osp/statesstandards.html.

Most OSHA offices have compliance assistance specialists to help employers and workers comply with OSHA standards. For details call 1-800-321-OSHA (6742) or visit: www.osha.gov/htm/RAmap.html.

This is one in a series of informational fact sheets highlighting OSHA programs, policies or standards. It does not impose any new compliance requirements. For a comprehensive list of compliance requirements of OSHA standards or regulations, refer to Title 29 of the Code of Federal Regulations. This information will be made available to sensory-impaired individuals upon request. The voice phone is (202) 693-1999; teletypewriter (TTY) number: (877) 889-5627.

For assistance, contact us. We can help. It's confidential.

U.S. Department of Labor
www.osha.gov (800) 321-OSHA (6742)

DOC FS-3662 05/2013

OSHA® FactSheet

Reducing Falls in Construction: Safe Use of Job-made Wooden Ladders

Workers who use job-made wooden ladders risk permanent injury or death from falls and electrocutions. These hazards can be eliminated or substantially reduced by following good safety practices. This fact sheet lists some of the hazards workers may encounter while working on **job-made wooden ladders** and explains what employers and workers can do to reduce injuries. OSHA's requirements for job-made ladders are in Subpart X—Stairways and Ladders of OSHA's Construction standards.

What is a Job-made Wooden Ladder?

A job-made wooden ladder is a ladder constructed at the construction site. It is not commercially-manufactured. A job-made wooden ladder provides access to and from a work area. It is not intended to serve as a work platform. These ladders are temporary, and are used only until a particular phase of work is completed or until permanent stairways or fixed ladders are installed. A 24-ft. job-made ladder built to the American National Standards Institute (ANSI) A14.4-2009 non-mandatory guidelines is shown below.

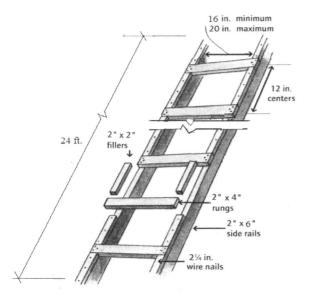

Figure 1: Single-Cleat Ladder

Training Requirements

Employers must provide a training program for employees using ladders and stairways. The training must enable each worker to recognize ladder-related hazards and to use ladders properly to minimize hazards.

Constructing a Safe Job-made Wooden Ladder

Side rails:

*   Use construction-grade lumber for all components.
*   Side rails of single-cleat ladders up to 24 ft. (7.3 m) long should be made with at least 2 in. (3.8 cm) x 6 in. (14 cm) nominal stock lumber.
*   Side rails should be continuous, unless splices are the same strength as a continuous rail of equal length.
*   The width of single-rung ladders should be at least 16 in. (41 cm), but not more than 20 in. (51 cm) between rails measured inside to inside.
*   Rails should extend above the top landing between 36 in. (91.5 cm) and 42 in. (1.1 m) to provide a handhold for mounting and dismounting, and cleats must be eliminated above the landing level.
*   Side rails of ladders which could contact energized electrical equipment should be made using nonconductive material. Keep ladders free of any slippery materials.
*   Only put ladders on a stable and level surface that is not slippery.

Cleats:

*   Cleats should be equally spaced 12 inches on center from the top of one cleat to the top of the next cleat.
*   Cleats should be fastened to each rail with three 12d common wire nails which are nailed directly onto the smaller surfaces of the side rails.
*   Making cuts in the side rails to receive the cleats is not advisable.
*   Cleats should be at least 1 in. (2.5 cm) x 4 in. (8.9 cm) for ladders 16 ft. (41 cm) to 24 ft. (7.3 m) in length.

Filler Blocks:

- Filler should be 2 in. (3.8 cm) x 2 in. (3.8 cm) wood strips.
- Insert filler between cleats.
- Nail filler at the bottom of each side rail first. Nail the ends of a cleat to each side rail with three 12d common nails. One nail is placed 1-1/2 inch in from each end of the filler block.
- Nail the next two fillers and cleat, and then repeat. The ladder is complete when filler is nailed at the top of each rail.
- Make all side rails, rungs and fillers before the ladder is assembled.

Inspecting Ladders

- A competent person must visually inspect job-made ladders for defects on a periodic basis and after any occurrence that could affect their safe use.
- Defects to look for include: structural damage, broken/split side rails (front and back), missing cleats/steps, and parts/labels painted over.
- Ladders should be free of oil, grease and other slipping hazards.

**PLAN.
PROVIDE.
TRAIN.**

Three simple steps to prevent falls.

Safe Ladder Use—DO:

To prevent workers from being injured from falls from ladders, employers are encouraged to adopt the following practices:

- Secure the ladder's base so that it does not move.
- Smooth the wood surface of the ladder to reduce injuries to workers from punctures or lacerations and to prevent snagging of clothing.
- Use job-made wooden ladders with spliced side rails at an angle so that the horizontal distance from the top support to the foot of the ladder is one-eighth the working length of the ladder.
- Ensure that job-made wooden ladders can support at least four times the maximum intended load.
- Only use ladders for the purpose for which they were designed.
- Only put ladders on stable and level surfaces unless secured to prevent accidental movement.
- Ensure that the worker faces the ladder when climbing up and down.
- Maintain a 3-point contact (two hands and a foot, or two feet and a hand) when climbing a ladder.
- Keep ladders free of any slippery materials.
- Maintain good housekeeping in the areas around the top and bottom of ladders.

Safe Ladder Use—DO NOT:

- Paint a ladder with nontransparent coatings.
- Carry any object or load that could cause the worker to lose balance and fall.
- Subject a job-made wooden ladder to excessive loads or impact tests.

OSHA standard: **29 CFR 1926 Subpart X**—Stairways and Ladders

American National Standards Institute standard: **ANSI A14.4-1979, ANSI A14.4-2009**

Employers constructing job-made ladders must follow the ladder requirements set forth in 29 C.F.R. 1926 Subpart X. They are encouraged to consult the non-mandatory guidelines set forth in ANSI A.14.4-1979— Safety Requirements for Job-Made Ladders (referenced in Appendix A to Subpart X of Part 1926—Ladders) and ANSI A.14.4-2009—Safety Requirements for Job-Made Wooden Ladders.

State plan guidance: States with OSHA-approved state plans may have additional requirements for avoiding falls from ladders. For more information on these requirements, please visit: www.osha.gov/dcsp/ osp/statesstandards.html.

Most OSHA offices have compliance assistance specialists to help employers and workers comply with OSHA standards. For details call 1-800-321-OSHA (6742) or visit: www.osha.gov/htm/RAmap.html.

OSHA® Occupational Safety and Health Administration

**U.S. Department of Labor
www.osha.gov (800) 321-OSHA (6742)**

DOC FS-3661 05/2013

Name: _____   Date: _____

Knowledge Check: Stairways and Ladders

1. When portable ladders are used for access to an upper landing surface, how many feet above the upper landing must the side rails extend?
   a. 2 feet
   b. 3 feet
   c. 4 feet
   d. 5 feet

2. You can use a metal ladder around power lines or exposed energized electrical equipment.
   a. True, but ONLY if there is no other option to get the work done.
   b. False, you should NEVER use a metal ladder in this circumstance.

3. Handrails must be able to withstand, without failure, how many pounds of weight applied within 2 inches of the top edge in any direction or outward direction?
   a. 300 pounds
   b. 250 pounds
   c. 200 pounds
   d. 175 pounds

4. Stairways that have four or more risers MUST have a stair rail.
   a. True
   b. False

5. A non-self-supporting ladder should be set up at _____ (horizontal distance/working length of ladder).
   a. 90 degree angle
   b. 30 degree angle
   c. 1:2 angle
   d. 1:4 angle

Tools – hand and power

Restraint Device on Power Press

Amputations

What are the sources of amputations in the workplace?

Amputations are some of the most serious and debilitating workplace injuries. They are widespread and involve a variety of activities and equipment. Amputations occur most often when workers operate unguarded or inadequately safeguarded mechanical power presses, power press brakes, powered and non-powered conveyors, printing presses, roll-forming and roll-bending machines, food slicers, meat grinders, meat-cutting band saws, drill presses, and milling machines as well as shears, grinders, and slitters. These injuries also happen during materials handling activities and when using forklifts and doors as well as trash compactors and powered and non-powered hand tools. Besides normal operation, the following activities involving stationary machines also expose workers to potential amputation hazards: setting-up, threading, preparing, adjusting, cleaning, lubricating, and maintaining machines as well as clearing jams.

What types of machine components are hazardous?

The following types of mechanical components present amputation hazards:

- **Point of operation**—the area of a machine where it performs work on material.

- **Power-transmission apparatuses**—flywheels, pulleys, belts, chains, couplings, spindles, cams, and gears in addition to connecting rods and other machine components that transmit energy.

- **Other moving parts**—machine components that move during machine operation such as reciprocating, rotating, and transverse moving parts as well as auxiliary machine parts.

What kinds of mechanical motion are hazardous?

All mechanical motion is potentially hazardous. In addition to in-running nip points ("pinch points")—which occur when two parts move together and at least one moves in a rotary or circular motion that gears, rollers, belt drives, and pulleys generate—the following are the most common types of hazardous mechanical motion:

- **Rotating**—circular movement of couplings, cams, clutches, flywheels, and spindles as well as shaft ends and rotating collars that may grip clothing or otherwise force a body part into a dangerous location.

- **Reciprocating**—back-and-forth or up-and-down action that may strike or entrap a worker between a moving part and a fixed object.

- **Transversing**—movement in a straight, continuous line that may strike or catch a worker in a pinch or shear point created between the moving part and a fixed object.

- **Cutting**—action generated during sawing, boring, drilling, milling, slicing, and slitting.

- **Punching**—motion resulting when a machine moves a slide (ram) to stamp or blank metal or other material.

- **Shearing**—movement of a powered slide or knife during metal trimming or shearing.

- **Bending**—action occurring when power is applied to a slide to draw or form metal or other materials.

Are there any OSHA standards that cover amputation hazards in the workplace?

Yes. The Occupational Safety and Health Administration (OSHA) has the following standards in *Title 29 of the Code of Federal Regulations* (*CFR*) to protect workers from amputations in the workplace:

- 29 *CFR* Part 1910 Subparts O and P cover machinery and machine guarding.

- 29 *CFR* 1926 Subpart I covers hand tools and powered tools.

- 29 *CFR* Part 1928 Subpart D covers agricultural equipment.

- 29 *CFR* Part 1915 Subparts C, H, and J; 29 *CFR* Part 1917 Subparts B, C, and G; and 29 *CFR* Part 1918 Subparts F, G, and H cover maritime operations.

What can employers do to help protect workers from amputations?

You should be able to recognize, identify, manage, and control amputation hazards commonly found in the workplace such as those caused by mechanical components of machinery, the mechanical motion that occurs in or near these components, and the activities that workers perform during mechanical operation.

Work practices, employee training, and administrative controls can help prevent and control amputation hazards. Machine safeguarding with the following equipment is the best way to control amputations caused by stationary machinery:

- **Guards** provide physical barriers that prevent access to hazardous areas. They should be secure and strong, and workers should not be able to bypass, remove, or tamper with them. Guards should not obstruct the operator's view or prevent employees from working.

- **Devices** help prevent contact with points of operation and may replace or supplement guards. Devices can interrupt the normal cycle of the machine when the operator's hands are at the point of operation, prevent the operator from reaching into the point of operation, or withdraw the operator's hands if they approach the point of operation when the machine cycles. They must allow safe lubrication and maintenance and not create hazards or interfere with normal machine operation. In addition, they should be secure, tamper-resistant, and durable.

You are responsible for safeguarding machines and should consider this need when purchasing machinery. New machinery is usually available with safeguards installed by the manufacturer. You can also purchase appropriate safeguards separately or build them in-house.

Are certain jobs particularly hazardous for some employees?

Yes. Under the *Fair Labor Standards Act*, the Secretary of Labor has designated certain non-farm jobs as especially hazardous for employees under the age of 18. These workers generally are prohibited from operating band saws, circular saws, guillotine shears, punching and shearing machines, meatpacking or meat-processing machines, paper products machines, woodworking machines, metal-forming machines, and meat slicers.

How can I get more information?

You can find more information about amputations, including the full text of OSHA's standards, on OSHA's website at **www.osha.gov**. In addition, publications explaining the subject of amputations in greater detail are available from OSHA. *Concepts and Techniques of Machine Safeguarding* (OSHA 3067) and *Control of Hazardous Energy (Lockout/Tagout)* (OSHA 3120) are available on OSHA's website. For other information about machine guarding see http://www.osha-slc.gov/SLTC/machineguarding/index.html.

A Guide for Protecting Workers from Woodworking Hazards (OSHA 3157) is available either on OSHA's website at **www.osha.gov** or from the Superintendent of Documents, P.O. Box 371954, Pittsburgh, PA 15250-7954, or phone (202) 512-1800, or online at http://bookstore.gpo.gov/index.html.

To file a complaint by phone, report an emergency, or get OSHA advice, assistance, or products, contact your nearest OSHA office under the "U.S. Department of Labor" listing in your phone book, or call us toll-free at **(800) 321-OSHA (6742)**; teletypewriter (TTY) number is (877) 889-5627. To file a complaint online or obtain more information on OSHA federal and state programs, visit OSHA's website at **www.osha.gov**.

This is one in a series of informational fact sheets highlighting OSHA programs, policies, or standards. It does not impose any new compliance requirements or carry the force of legal opinion. For compliance requirements of OSHA standards or regulations, refer to *Title 29 of the Code of Federal Regulations*. This information will be made available to sensory-impaired individuals upon request. Voice phone: (202) 693-1999. See also OSHA's website at **www.osha.gov.**

U.S. Department of Labor
Occupational Safety and Health Administration
2002

Name: _____ 　　　　Date: _____

Knowledge Check: Tools – Hand and Power

1. Which of the following is an example of an unsafe practice regarding the use of tools?
    a. Keeping cutting tools sharp
    b. Wearing eye and face protection while operating a grinder
    c. Using a screwdriver to carve or cut wood
    d. Following manufacturer's instructions when using a tool

2. Which term describes a tool that is powered by compressed air?
    a. Hydraulic
    b. Powder-actuated
    c. Electrical
    d. Pneumatic

3. Which of the following actions may expose workers to electrical shock hazards and should be avoided?
    a. Removing the grounding pin on a three-prong plug
    b. Using double-insulated tools
    c. Using a grounded adaptor to accommodate a two-prong receptacle
    d. Removing damaged tools from service and tagging them "Do Not Use"

4. Which of the following statements about guarding techniques is true?
    a. Guard the point of operation, in-running nip points, and rotating parts of tools.
    b. Remove guard from tool while it is in use, then replace when the job is completed.
    c. Adjust guard on abrasive wheel to allow maximum exposure of the wheel surface.
    d. Wear PPE because guards will not protect operator from flying chips and sparks or moving parts of tools.

5. Employers must satisfy all of the following requirements, except:
    a. Provide PPE necessary to protect employees who are operating hand and power tools and are exposed to hazards.
    b. Comply with OSHA training and inspection standards related to hand and power tools.
    c. Determine which manufacturer's requirements and recommendations for a tool shall be followed or ignored.
    d. Do not issue or permit the use of unsafe hand tools.

Health hazards in construction

OSHA FactSheet

Protecting Workers from Asbestos Hazards

Cleaning up after a flood requires hundreds of workers to renovate and repair, or tear down and dispose of, damaged or destroyed structures and materials. However, repair, renovation, and demolition operations often generate airborne asbestos, a mineral fiber that can cause chronic lung disease or cancer. The Occupational Safety and Health Administration (OSHA) has developed regulations designed to protect cleanup workers from asbestos hazards.

How You Can Become Exposed to Asbestos

Before it was known that inhalation of asbestos fibers causes several deadly diseases—including asbestosis, a progressive and often fatal lung disease, and lung and other cancers—asbestos was used in a large number of building materials and other products because of its strength, flame resistance, and insulating properties. Asbestos was used in asbestos-cement pipe and sheeting, floor and roofing felts, dry wall, floor tiles, spray on ceiling coatings, and packing materials. When buildings containing these materials are renovated or torn down, or when the asbestos- containing materials themselves are disturbed, minute asbestos fibers may be released into the air. The fibers are so small that they often cannot be seen with the naked eye; the fact that you can inhale these fibers without knowing it makes asbestos an even more dangerous hazard.

OSHA's Standards for Asbestos

The work of flood cleanup personnel involves the repair, renovation, removal, demolition, or salvage of flood-damaged structures and materials. Such materials may contain or be covered with asbestos, and cleanup personnel are protected by OSHA's construction industry asbestos standard
(Title 29 Code of Federal Regulations (CFR), Part 1926.1101). This standard requires employers to follow various procedures to protect their employees from inhaling asbestos fibers. The standard contains many requirements that vary depending on the kind of work being undertaken, the amount of asbestos in the air, and other factors. You and your employer can obtain a copy of this standard and the booklet, Asbestos Standards for Construction (OSHA 3096) describing how to comply with it, from OSHA Publications, P.O. Box 37535, Washington, DC 20013-7535, (202) 693- 1888(phone), or (202) 693-2498(fax); or visit OSHA's website at www.osha.gov.

Major Elements of OSHA's Asbestos Standard

The following include some of the major requirements of the asbestos standard. For complete information on all requirements, see 29 CFR 1926.1101.

- A permissible exposure limit (PEL) of 0.1 fiber of asbestos per cubic centimeter of air as averaged over an 8-hour period, with an excursion limit of 1.0 asbestos fibers per cubic centimeter over a 30-minute period.
- Requirements for an initial exposure assessment to ascertain expected exposures during that work operation, and periodic expo-sure monitoring in certain instances.
- Use of engineering controls, to the extent feasible, to meet the PEL. Where this is not possible, engineering controls must be used to reduce exposures to the lowest levels possible and then supplemented by the use of appropriate respiratory protection.

- Use of regulated areas to limit access to locations where asbestos concentrations may be dangerously high.
- No smoking, eating, or drinking in asbestos-regulated areas.
- Requirements for warning signs and caution labels to identify and communicate the presence of hazards and hazardous materials; recordkeeping; and medical surveillance.

Additional Information

For more information on this, and other health-related issues impacting workers, visit OSHA's Web site at www.osha.gov.

This is one in a series of informational fact sheets highlighting OSHA programs, policies or standards. It does not impose any new compliance requirements. For a comprehensive list of compliance requirements of OSHA standards or regulations, refer to Title 29 of the Code of Federal Regulations. This information will be made available to sensory impaired individuals upon request. The voice phone is (202) 693-1999; teletypewriter (TTY) number: (877) 889-5627.

For more complete information:

OSHA Occupational Safety and Health Administration

U.S. Department of Labor
www.osha.gov
(800) 321-OSHA

DSTM 9/2005

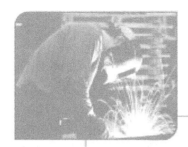

OSHA **FACT** Sheet

Crystalline Silica Exposure
Health Hazard Information

What is crystalline silica?

Crystalline silica is a basic component of soil, sand, granite, and many other minerals. Quartz is the most common form of crystalline silica. Cristobalite and tridymite are two other forms of crystalline silica. All three forms may become respirable size particles when workers chip, cut, drill, or grind objects that contain crystalline silica.

What are the hazards of crystalline silica?

Silica exposure remains a serious threat to nearly 2 million U.S. workers, including more than 100,000 workers in high risk jobs such as abrasive blasting, foundry work, stonecutting, rock drilling, quarry work and tunneling. The seriousness of the health hazards associated with silica exposure is demonstrated by the fatalities and disabling illnesses that continue to occur in sandblasters and rockdrillers. Crystalline silica has been classified as a human lung carcinogen. Additionally, breathing crystalline silica dust can cause **silicosis**, which in severe cases can be disabling, or even fatal. The respirable silica dust enters the lungs and causes the formation of scar tissue, thus reducing the lungs' ability to take in oxygen. There is no cure for silicosis. Since silicosis affects lung function, it makes one more susceptible to lung infections like **tuberculosis.** In addition, smoking causes lung damage and adds to the damage caused by breathing silica dust.

What are the symptoms of silicosis?

Silicosis is classified into three types: chronic/classic, accelerated, and acute.

Chronic/classic silicosis, the most common, occurs after 15–20 years of moderate to low exposures to respirable crystalline silica. Symptoms associated with chronic silicosis may or may not be obvious; therefore, workers need to have a chest x-ray to determine if there is lung damage. As the disease progresses, the worker may experience shortness of breath upon exercising and have clinical signs of poor oxygen/carbon dioxide exchange. In the later stages, the worker may experience fatigue, extreme shortness of breath, chest pain, or respiratory failure.

Accelerated silicosis can occur after 5–10 years of high exposures to respirable crystalline silica. Symptoms include severe shortness of breath, weakness, and weight loss. The onset of symptoms takes longer than in acute silicosis.

Acute silicosis occurs after a few months or as long as 2 years following exposures to extremely high concentrations of respirable crystalline silica. Symptoms of acute silicosis include severe disabling shortness of breath, weakness, and weight loss, which often leads to death.

Where are construction workers exposed to crystalline silica?

Exposure occurs during many different construction activities. The most severe exposures generally occur during abrasive blasting with sand to remove paint and rust from bridges, tanks, concrete structures, and other surfaces. Other construction activities that may result in severe exposure include: jack hammering, rock/well drilling, concrete mixing, concrete drilling, brick and concrete block cutting and sawing, tuck pointing, tunneling operations.

Where are general industry employees exposed to crystalline silica dust?

The most severe exposures to crystalline silica result from abrasive blasting, which is done to clean and smooth irregularities from molds, jewelry, and foundry castings, finish tombstones, etch or frost glass, or remove paint, oils, rust, or dirt form objects needing to be repainted or treated. Other exposures to silica dust occur in cement and brick manufacturing, asphalt pavement manufacturing, china and ceramic manufacturing and the tool and die, steel and foundry industries. Crystalline silica is used in manufacturing, household abrasives, adhesives, paints, soaps, and glass. Additionally, crystalline silica exposures occur in the maintenance, repair and replacement of refractory brick furnace linings.

In the maritime industry, shipyard employees are exposed to silica primarily in abrasive blasting operations to remove paint and clean and prepare steel hulls, bulkheads, decks, and tanks for paints and coatings.

How is OSHA addressing exposure to crystalline silica?

OSHA has an established Permissible Exposure Limit, or PEL, which is the maximum amount of crystalline silica to which workers may be exposed during an 8-hour work shift (29 *CFR* 1926.55, 1910.1000). OSHA also requires hazard

144

communication training for workers exposed to crystalline silica, and requires a respirator protection program until engineering controls are implemented. Additionally, OSHA has a National Emphasis Program (NEP) for Crystalline Silica exposure to identify, reduce, and eliminate health hazards associated with occupational exposures.

What can employers/employees do to protect against exposures to crystalline silica?

- Replace crystalline silica materials with safer substitutes, whenever possible.

- Provide engineering or administrative controls, where feasible, such as local exhaust ventilation, and blasting cabinets. Where necessary to reduce exposures below the PEL, use protective equipment or other protective measures.

- Use all available work practices to control dust exposures, such as water sprays.

- Wear only a N95 NIOSH certified respirator, if respirator protection is required. Do not alter the respirator. Do not wear a tight-fitting respirator with a beard or mustache that prevents a good seal between the respirator and the face.

- Wear only a Type CE abrasive-blast supplied-air respirator for abrasive blasting.

- Wear disposable or washable work clothes and shower if facilities are available. Vacuum the dust from your clothes or change into clean clothing before leaving the work site.

- Participate in training, exposure monitoring, and health screening and surveillance programs to monitor any adverse health effects caused by crystalline silica exposures.

- Be aware of the operations and job tasks creating crystalline silica exposures in your workplace environment and know how to protect yourself.

- Be aware of the health hazards related to exposures to crystalline silica. Smoking adds to the lung damage caused by silica exposures.

- Do not eat, drink, smoke, or apply cosmetics in areas where crystalline silica dust is present. Wash your hands and face outside of dusty areas before performing any of these activities.

- Remember: If it's silica, it's not just dust.

How can I get more information on safety and health?

OSHA has various publications, standards, technical assistance, and compliance tools to help you, and offers extensive assistance through workplace consultation, voluntary protection programs, strategic partnerships, alliances, state plans, grants, training, and education. OSHA's *Safety and Health Program Management Guidelines* (*Federal Register* 54:3904-3916, January 26, 1989) detail elements critical to the development of a successful safety and health management system. This and other information are available on OSHA's website.

- For one free copy of OSHA publications, send a self-addressed mailing label to OSHA Publications Office, 200 Constitution Avenue N.W., N-3101, Washington, DC 20210; or send a request to our fax at (202) 693–2498, or call us toll-free at (800) 321–OSHA.

- To order OSHA publications online at **www.osha.gov**, go to **Publications** and follow the instructions for ordering.

- To file a complaint by phone, report an emergency, or get OSHA advice, assistance, or products, contact your nearest OSHA office under the U.S. Department of Labor listing in your phone book, or call toll-free at **(800) 321– OSHA (6742)**. The teletypewriter (TTY) number is (877) 889–5627.

- To file a complaint online or obtain more information on OSHA federal and state programs, visit OSHA's website.

This is one in a series of informational fact sheets highlighting OSHA programs, policies, or standards. It does not impose any new compliance requirements. For a comprehensive list of compliance requirements of OSHA standards or regulations, refer to *Title 29 of the Code of Federal Regulations*. This information will be made available to sensory-impaired individuals upon request. The voice phone is (202) 693–1999. See also OSHA's website at **www.osha.gov**.

OSHA
Occupational Safety
and Health Administration
U.S. Department of Labor
2002

OSHA FactSheet

Protecting Workers from Lead Hazards

Cleaning up after a flood requires hundreds of workers to renovate and repair, or tear down and dispose of, damaged or destroyed structures and materials. Repair, renovation and demolition operations often generate dangerous airborne concentrations of lead, a metal that can cause damage to the nervous system, kidneys, blood forming organs, and reproductive system if inhaled or ingested in danger-ous quantities. The Occupational Safety and Health Administration (OSHA) has developed regulations designed to protect workers involved in construction activities from the hazards of lead exposure.

How You Can Become Exposed to Lead

Lead is an ingredient in thousands of products widely used throughout industry, including lead-based paints, lead solder, electrical fittings and conduits, tank linings, plumbing fixtures, and many metal alloys. Although many uses of lead have been banned, lead-based paints continue to be used on bridges, railways, ships, and other steel structures because of its rust- and corrosion-inhibiting properties. Also, many homes were painted with lead-containing paints. Significant lead exposures can also occur when paint is removed from surfaces previously covered with lead-based paint.

Operations that can generate lead dust and fumes include:

• Demolition of structures;
• Flame-torch cutting;
• Welding;
• Use of heat guns, sanders, scrapers, or grinders to remove lead paint; and
• Abrasive blasting of steel structures

OSHA has regulations governing construc-tion worker exposure to lead. Employers of construction workers engaged in the repair, renovation, removal, demolition, and salvage of flood-damaged structures and materials are responsible for the development and implementation of a worker protection program in accordance with Title 29 Code of Federal Regulations (CFR), Part 1926.62. This program is essential to minimize worker risk of lead exposure. Construction projects vary in their scope and potential for exposing workers to lead and other hazards. Many projects involve only limited exposure, such as the removal of paint from a few interior residential surfaces, while others may involve substantial exposures. Employers must be in compliance with OSHA's lead standard at all times. A copy of the standard and a brochure— Lead in Construction (OSHA 3142) —describing how to comply with it, are avail-able from OSHA Publications, P.O. Box 37535, Washington, D.C. 20013-7535, (202) 693-1888(phone), or (202) 693-2498(fax); or visit OSHA's website at www.osha.gov.

Major Elements of OSHA's Lead Standard

• A permissible exposure limit (PEL) of 50 micrograms of lead per cubic meter of air, as averaged over an 8-hour period.
• Requirements that employers use engineering controls and work practices, where feasible, to reduce worker exposure.
• Requirements that employees observe good personal hygiene practices, such as washing hands before eating and taking a shower before leaving the worksite.
• Requirements that employees be provided with protective clothing and, where necessary, with respiratory protection accordance with 29 CFR 1910.134.

• A requirement that employees exposed to high levels of lead be enrolled in a medical surveillance program.

Additional Information

For more information on this, and other health-related issues impacting workers, visit OSHA's Web site at www.osha.gov.

This is one in a series of informational fact sheets highlighting OSHA programs, policies or standards. It does not impose any new compliance requirements. For a comprehensive list of compliance requirements of OSHA standards or regulations, refer to Title 29 of the Code of Federal Regulations. This information will be made available to sensory impaired individuals upon request. The voice phone is (202) 693-1999; teletypewriter (TTY) number: (877) 889-5627.

For more complete information:

OSHA Occupational Safety and Health Administration

U.S. Department of Labor
www.osha.gov
(800) 321-OSHA

DSTM 11/2005

Name: _____   Date: _____

Knowledge Check: Health Hazards in Construction

1. Which of the following is a common type of health hazard?
    a. Chemical hazards
    b. Economic hazards
    c. Electrical hazards
    d. Fall hazards

2. Which of the following is an example of a physical health hazard?
    a. Asbestos
    b. Noise
    c. Silica
    d. Lead

3. Which is an appropriate engineering control for protection against noise exposures?
    a. Audiograms
    b. Earplugs
    c. Increasing distance between source
    d. Constructing sound barriers

4. Which is a requirement of the employer?
    a. Determine if workers exposures exceed OSHA PELs
    b. Perform medical evaluations on all employees
    c. Develop silica training programs for all employees
    d. Provide workers with steel-toed boots

Books in the OSHA Outreach Training Program Series

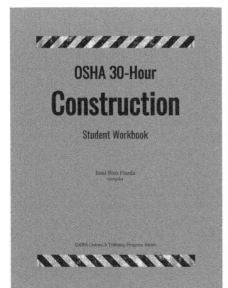

OSHA 30-Hour Construction Student Workbook (ISBN-13: 978-1975997830)

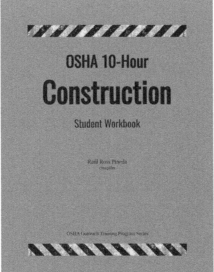

OSHA 10-Hour construction Student Workbook (ISBN-13: 978-1546484363)

OSHA 10-Hour General Industry; Student Workbook (ISBN-13: 978-1979408592)

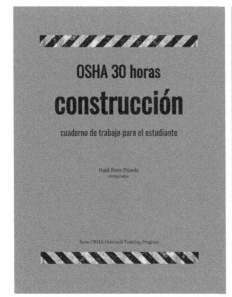

OSHA 30 horas construcción cuaderno de trabajo para el estudiante (ISBN-13: 978-1977837479)

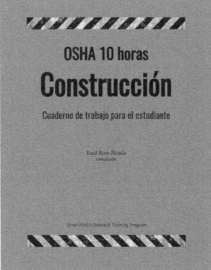

OSHA 10 horas construcción cuaderno de trabajo para el estudiante (ISBN-13: 978-1974103553)

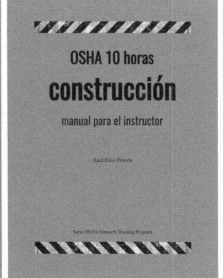

OSHA 10 horas construcción: manual para el instructor

(coming soon)

Search by author, title or ISBN in your favorite online bookstore

Made in the USA
Las Vegas, NV
05 February 2022